KOL NIDREI

KOL NIDREI

Its Origin, Development, and Significance

Stuart Weinberg Gershon

JASON ARONSON INC
Northvale, New Jersey
London

The author gratefully acknowledges permission to reprint the following:

The music of Aaron Beer, S. Naumbourg, L. Lewandowski, Abrahams Baer. From "The Kol Nidre Tune," by A. Z. Idelsohn, HEBREW UNION COLLEGE ANNUAL 8–9, 1931–1932. Copyright © 1932 Union of American Hebrew Congregations. Reprinted by permission of *Hebrew Union College Annual.*

From PRAYERS FOR THE DAY OF ATONEMENT: ACCORDING TO THE CUSTOM OF THE SPANISH AND PORTUGUESE JEWS, ed. and trans. David de Sola Pool. Copyright © 1939 David de Sola Pool. Reprinted by permission of the Union of Sephardic Congregations.

From MACHZOR LAYAMIM HANORAIM, ed. Daniel Goldschmidt. Copyright © 1970 Leo Baeck Institute. Courtesy of the Leo Baeck Institute, Inc., New York.

This book was set in 11 pt. Goudy by Alpha Graphics of Pittsfield, New Hampshire, and printed by Haddon Craftsmen in Scranton, Pennsylvania.

Library of Congress Cataloging-in-Publication Data

Gershon, Stuart Weinberg.
    Kol nidrei : its origin, development, and significance / Stuart Weinberg Gershon.
      p.   cm.
    Includes bibliographical references and index.
    ISBN 1-56821-200-3
    1. Kol nidrei. 2. Yom Kippur—Liturgy. 3. Judaism—Liturgy.
    4. Vows (Jewish law) I. Title.
    BM670.K6G47   1994
    296.4'32—dc 20   93-50085

Manufactured in the United States of America. Jason Aronson Inc. offers books and cassettes. For information and catalog write to Jason Aronson Inc., 230 Livingston Street, Northvale, New Jersey 07647.

Contents

PART IV: CONCLUSION

Acknowledgments

The act of personal discovery is a heady feeling. The only experience that surpasses it is the joy that comes from sharing the enterprise of research and learning with my teachers and mentors.

A special word of heartfelt gratitude goes to my mentor and friend, Dr. Lawrence A. Hoffman, from whom I have learned so much about the scholarly enterprise, homiletics, and the craft of writing.

I would like also to express my profound appreciation to several teachers for their invaluable assistance at various stages of this project: Dr. David Sperling, Dr. Richard White, Rabbi Manuel Gold, Dr. Baruch Levine, Dr. David Kraemer, Rabbi Geoffrey Goldberg, and Dr. Menachem Schmelzer. Thank you for your insights, your enthusiasm for my work, and for those exciting moments of collegiality.

My word of thanks goes also to Rabbi Steven Conn and Hal Hirschfield, my *chevrutah* buddies, who helped me to master the rabbinic texts I cherish so much.

Acharon, acharon, chaviv. Words cannot express my deepest gratitude to Diana Knight. Without her abiding love, inspirational support, and incredible patience, this book would not have been completed. To you, dear heart, I dedicate this work.

Introduction

It is arguably the most famous, beloved, and emotionally powerful ritual in Judaism. Jews of every persuasion—from ultra-Orthodox to secular, from synagogue-affiliated to those only marginally Jewish—all find themselves drawn to synagogue on Yom Kippur eve to hear its words and melody.

Kol nidrei. For those who hear it chanted, it never fails to transport them to some deep, inner place. A place intermingled with tears and joy. Its words go directly to the heart.

Kol nidrei is a mystery and a paradox. A mystery because its author and precise date and place of origin are uncertain. A paradox because *kol nidrei* is not a prayer. It never once mentions God!

The place to begin to tell the true story of *kol nidrei* is with the words themselves:

> All vows, prohibitive vows, oaths, vows of dedication, *konam*-vows, *konas*-vows, and equivalent terms that we have vowed, sworn, declared, and imposed upon ourselves from this day of atonement until the next day of atonement, may it come upon us for good. Regarding them all, we regret them. Let them all be released, forgiven, erased, null and void. They are not valid nor are they in force. Our vows are not vows. Our prohibitive vows are not prohibitive vows. Our oaths are not oaths.

The *kol nidrei* text raises more questions than it answers. Why is it so dense with legal terminology? Why is *kol nidrei* so concerned to invalidate vows in advance of their inception? *Kol nidrei* appears to authorize a blanket absolution of all vows. Does that mean *kol nidrei* annuls one's marriage vows? Can it nullify one's testimony in a court of law? And what about the matter of intention? Does *kol nidrei* release vowers who intentionally failed to fulfill their vows?

In this book, we shall account for *kol nidrei*'s prominent place in the liturgy for Yom Kippur, explain what the disavowal of vows has to do with this most sacred of Jewish days, and offer suggestions about the source of *kol nidrei*'s unrivaled ritual power.

I
VOWS IN ANTIQUITY

1

Vows in the Biblical Period

The concept of vows in classical Judaism cannot be understood without beginning at its source, the Hebrew Bible. The Hebrew Bible set the framework for the subsequent understanding and treatment of vows in postbiblical Judaism.

Vows are frequently mentioned in the Hebrew Bible. Whereas an oath can be defined as a solemn promise, a vow (from the Latin *votum*) involves "something given." The Hebrew word for vow is *neder*, from the root meaning "to set apart for sacred use."[1] A vow in the Hebrew Bible denoted the dedication of an animal, an object, or a person to God. Conversely, it may also have involved abstinence from an item in honor of God.[2]

Vows were pronounced at sacred sites such as temples or altars. It appears to have been customary to return to the site where the vow was made when the time came to fulfill it.[3] Three types of vows occur

---

1. Roland de Vaux, *Ancient Israel: Its Life and Institutions* (London: Darton, Longman & Todd, 1961), 465. The Ugaritic root *pla* means "something set aside."

2. John Sturdy, *Numbers*, The Cambridge Bible Commentary (London: Cambridge University Press, 1976), 210; *The Encyclopedia of the Jewish Religion*, 1966 ed., s.v. "Vows and Oaths."

3. Baruch A. Levine, *In the Presence of the Lord* (Leiden: E. J. Brill, 1974), 45 n. 117.

3

in the Hebrew Bible: vows of dedication, vows of prohibition, and Nazirite vows.[4]

Vows of dedication (*nidrei hekdesh*) involved the dedication of an animal sacrifice or some other gift to God.[5] Such vows were frequently offered in thanksgiving for divine kindness already received:

> How can I repay the LORD for all His bounties to me? I raise the cup of deliverance and invoke the name of the LORD. I will pay my vows to the LORD in the presence of all His people (Psalm 116:12–14).

and

> I must pay my vow to You, O God; I will render thank offerings to You. For You have saved me from death, my foot from stumbling, that I may walk before God in the light of life (Psalm 56:13–14).[6]

Vows of dedication were also made in times of danger or special need when God's help was desperately sought:[7]

> I enter your house with burnt offerings; I pay my vows to You, that my lips pronounced, that my mouth uttered in my distress (Psalm 66:13).

---

4. Martin Noth, *Numbers: A Commentary*, The Old Testament Library (Philadelphia: Westminster Press, 1968), 224–225; *Harper's Bible Dictionary*, 8th ed., s.v. "Vow."

5. Chanoch Albeck, *Shishah Sidrei Mishnah, Seder Nashim, Masekhet Nedarim* (Jerusalem: Mossad Bialik), 137; hence, the term *neder* may denote not only the vow itself, but the votive offering connected to it. Cf. Leviticus 7:16, 22:21, 27:2; Numbers 15:3, 29:39, Deuteronomy 12:6,11,17,26; 1 Samuel 1:21.

6. See also Psalm 65:2–3 and Jonah 2:10.

7. Philip J. Budd, *Numbers*, Word Biblical Commentary, vol. 5 (Waco, TX: Word Book), 322.

and

> O God, You have heard my vows; grant the request of those who
> fear Your name. . . . So I will sing hymns to Your name forever,
> as I fulfill my vows day after day (Psalm 61:6,9).

Vows of dedication were frequently conditional upon a favor
being granted by God.[8] The vower made a statement such that "if I
receive X benefit, I will do Y in return."

The most prominent vows in the Hebrew Bible are conditional
vows of dedication:

> Jacob then made a vow, saying, "If God remains with me, if He
> protects me on this journey that I am making, and gives me bread
> to eat and clothing to wear, and if I return safe to my father's
> house—the LORD shall be my God. And this stone, which I have
> set up as a pillar, shall be God's abode; and of all that You give
> me, I will set aside a tithe for You" (Genesis 28:20).

Conditional vows of dedication were also made by Israel (Numbers 21:2), Jepthah (Judges 11:30-31), Hannah (1 Samuel 1:11),
Absalom (2 Samuel 15:7–8), and Jonah's shipmates (Jonah 1:16).
These vows dedicated to God, respectively, a tithe, spoils of war, a
human sacrifice, a person for Temple service (cf. Proverbs 31:2), and
animal sacrifices.

Vows of prohibition (*nidrei issur*) involved voluntary abstinence
and self-affliction on the part of the vower.[9] Through an act of self-
sacrifice, the vower hoped to win God's favor or express gratitude for
it. Like vows of dedication, vows of abstinence could also be conditional or unconditional. Vows of prohibition are mentioned in Numbers 30 and nowhere else in the Hebrew Bible:[10]

---

8. de Vaux, *Ancient Israel*, 465.
9. Budd, *Numbers*, 322.
10. Budd, *Numbers*, 321; Noth, *Numbers*, 225.

If a man makes a vow to the LORD or takes an oath imposing a prohibition on himself [la'asor issar al nafsho], he shall not break his pledge; he must carry out all that has crossed his lips.

The verb asar comes from the Hebrew root "to bind." The noun form connotes a "binding obligation," specifically a "prohibition," and therefore refers to a vow of self-affliction or self-abnegation.[11]

The term issar occurs 13 times in Numbers 30:3–15. According to Snaith, the term issar

> is new with the P-tradition. Previously the word neder included all kinds of vows and pledges, but now neder involves the positive vow whereby a man binds himself to give something, whilst 'issar is the negative vow whereby a man binds himself to abstain from something.[12]

Unfortunately, Numbers 30 does not indicate the range of possible afflictions that would fall under the category of a prohibitive vow. The term la'anot nafesh (Numbers 30:14), "to afflict oneself," suggests, however, that any kind of self-mortification is involved. The phrase is frequently synonymous with fasting.[13]

Nazirite vows involved aspects of both vows of dedication and vows of prohibition. The word nazir, like the term neder, also meant "to set apart for sacred use."[14] A nazirite vow originally involved the unconditional dedication of a person to God for life, during which time the nazir abstained from wine (and all fermented grape drinks), the cutting of hair, and contact with the dead.

The Nazirite vow was regarded in the Hebrew Bible as a special and exceptional commitment.[15] Amos 2:11 placed the nazir on a par with the prophet. Samson (Judges 13:5) was destined by God to be a

---

11. Budd, *Numbers*, 322.

12. N. H. Snaith, ed., *Leviticus and Numbers*, The Century Bible (London: Thomas Nelson & Sons, 1967), 321.

13. Cf. Numbers 29:7; Leviticus 16:29, 23:26–29.

14. Sturdy, *Numbers*, 48.

15. Cf. Leviticus 22:21; 27:2; Numbers 6:2; 15:3,8.

nazir and Samuel (1 Samuel 1:11) was consecrated by his mother when he was yet unborn, as part of her prayer to overcome barrenness.

The rules of the Nazirite vow described in Numbers 6 are generally ascribed to the Priestly source and reflect the postexilic period:[16]

> The LORD spoke to Moses, saying, "Speak to the Israelites and say to them: If anyone, man or woman, explicitly utters a nazirite's vow, to set himself apart for the LORD, he shall abstain from wine and any other intoxicant; . . . no razor shall touch his head . . . he shall not go in where there is a dead person" (Numbers 6:1–8).

At this stage, the nazirate was open to anyone and for a specific period of time. Queen Helena of Adiabene (first century C.E.), for example, observed the Nazirite vow for twenty-one years, in gratitude for the safe return of her son from war.[17]

Deuteronomic sources made it abundantly clear that vows were a serious business that must be carried out:

> You must fulfill what has crossed your lips and perform what you have voluntarily vowed to the LORD your God, having made the promise with your own mouth (Deuteronomy 23:24).

This view was reiterated in Numbers 30, attributed to a later Priestly source:

> If a man makes a vow to the LORD or takes an oath imposing a prohibition upon himself, he shall not break his pledge; he must carry out all that has crossed his lips (Numbers 30:3).

At the same time, however, Numbers 30 established the principle of the revocation of vows (*hafarat nedarim*). Fathers had the power to revoke the vows of their daughters (as minors), and hus-

---

16. Noth, *Numbers*, 54; Budd, *Numbers*, 321–322.
17. M. *Nazir* 3:6.

bands had the power to disallow the vows of their wives, as long as they did so immediately upon hearing about them:[18]

> But if her father restrains her on the day he finds out, none of her vows or self-imposed prohibitions shall stand; and the LORD will absolve her, since her father restrained her (Numbers 30:6).

and

> But if her husband does annul them on the day he finds out, then nothing that has crossed her lips shall stand, whether vows or self-imposed obligations. Her husband has revoked them, and the LORD will absolve her. Every vow and every sworn obligation of self-denial may be upheld by her husband or annulled by her husband (Numbers 30: 13–14).

But the vows of widows and divorcees, like those of all adult males, could not be revoked by any other party:

> The vow of a widow or of a divorced woman, however, whatever she has imposed on herself, shall be binding upon her (Numbers 30:10).

Clearly legal in nature, the terminology of Numbers 30 is highly significant both for what it says and for what it does not. Numbers 30 recognizes the legitimacy of the *revocation* of vows (*hafarat nedarim*), but restricts its applicability to female minors and married women. It nowhere mentions the *nullification* of vows (*hatarat nedarim*). Indeed, there is no provision for the nullification of vows in the Hebrew Bible. It is a postbiblical phenomenon.

The distinction made here between *nullification* and *revocation* of vows is not merely one of semantics. As we shall discuss in Chap-

---

18. According to Snaith (*Leviticus and Numbers*, 323), the text sought to clarify that the rule is the same for betrothed women who had not yet gone to live with their husbands and women who already lived in their husbands' houses. So too Budd, *Numbers*, 323, and Sturdy, *Numbers*, 210.

ter Three, the rabbis would make a serious philosophical and legal distinction between *hatarat nedarim* and *hafarat nedarim*. While both procedures effected the same outcome, their legal powers and who had the authority to exercise them were quite different. Briefly put, fathers and husbands possessed the authority *lehafir*—that is, to revoke the vows of their daughters and wives whereby the vow that once existed continues to exist but has been rendered inoperative. In contrast, the sages did not possess the power to revoke a vow already in force, but only *lehatir*, to annul a vow that had not yet taken force. They resorted to a legal fiction consisting of the retroactive nullification of the vow *ab initio* (from the moment of its inception), whereby the vow that once existed no longer exists and had never existed. Consequently it had never taken force.

Since no other population besides female minors and married women has even the possibility of being released from their vows, biblical sources encourage people not to make vows at all:

> When you make a vow to the LORD your God, do not put off fulfilling it, for the LORD your God will require it of you, and you will have incurred guilt, whereas you will incur no guilt if you refrain from vowing (Deuteronomy 23:22–23).

and

> When you make a vow to God, do not delay to fulfill it. For He has no pleasure in fools; what you vow, fulfill. It is better not to vow at all than to vow and not fulfill (Ecclesiastes 5:3–4).[19]

Leviticus 27, however, describes a procedure by which people like the *nazir*, who had been dedicated through a vow to the service of God, could be released from the vow through a money payment:[20]

---

19. Cf. Proverbs 20:25.

20. Martin Noth, *Leviticus: A Commentary*, The Old Testament Library (Philadelphia: Westminster Press, 1965), 225; George Buchanan Gray, *Sacrifice in the Old Testament: Its Theory and Practice* (New York: Ktav, 1971), 33–40.

The LORD spoke to Moses, saying: Speak to the Israelite people
and say to them: When anyone explicitly vows to the LORD the
equivalent for a human being, the following scale shall apply: If
it is a male from twenty to sixty years of age, the equivalent is
fifty shekels of silver by the sanctuary weight; if it is a female, the
equivalent is thirty shekels. If the age is from five years to twenty
years, the equivalent is twenty shekels for a male and ten shekels for a female. If the age is from one month to five years, the
equivalent for a male is five shekels of silver, and the equivalent
for a female is three shekels of silver. If the age is sixty years or
over, the equivalent is fifteen shekels in the case of a male and
ten shekels for a female. But if one cannot afford the equivalent,
he shall be presented before the priest, and the priest shall assess
him; the priest shall assess him according to what the vower can
afford (Leviticus 27:1–8).

The amount of money owed to the Temple is based on the "value"
attributed to the age and sex of the person who is being redeemed.
Thus far, the term *neder* seems to be restricted to religious para-
meters, exclusively denoting a personal obligation made with God
whereby an individual takes upon oneself the burden of abstinence
or the dedication of a gift. Vows in the Hebrew Bible do not appear
to pertain to interpersonal commitments, such as commercial obligations. It shall become a matter of dispute in the Medieval period
as to whether *kol nidrei* had the power to annul solemn promises made
to others, or whether it was in fact limited to personal vows imposed
upon oneself. The Hebrew Bible records little of the role played by
vows in social discourse and magic. For those aspects of vows we must
turn to the *Mishnah* and to vows in the rabbinic period.

2
Vows in the Rabbinic Period

The nature and function of vows in the *Mishnah* have undergone significant legal development.[1] *Nidrei issur*, prohibitive vows, have been accorded a precise definition:

> A prohibitive vow is one in which a person prohibits a permissible item of his own to himself or to others, or someone else's item to himself.[2]

It may be recalled from the discussion in Chapter One that *nidrei hekdesh* involved the dedication of a gift (*korban*), consisting in an animal sacrifice, money, or some other object, but only to God. This aspect of the dedicatory vow has been retained in the mishnaic formula for prohibitive vows. The vower declared, "This item is prohib-

---

1. The *Mishnah* deals with *nidrei hekdesh*, vows of dedication, in *Seder Kodashim*. Our study of the history of *kol nidrei* proceeds along a different path, with the further development of *nidrei issur*, prohibitive vows.

2. Mordechai Rabinovitch, *The Mishnah, Seder Nashim, vol. II(a), Tractate Nedarim*, ArtScroll Mishnah Series (Brooklyn: Mesorah Publications, 1985), 1; Herbert Danby, *The Mishnah* (London: Oxford University Press, 1933), 794.

ited to me like a *korban*" or "*Korban* be the use of this item to me."[3]
The vower thereby prohibited the item from himself, usually food or
drink, as if it were an object dedicated to God.

Rabbinic vows (*nedarim*) and oaths (*shevuot*) differed in several
ways. One difference between a vow and an oath hinges on the subject
of interdiction.[4] An *oath* is a solemn promise to do or not do an action.
The focus of an oath obligates the person ("I swear . . ."). A *vow*, on
the other hand, is oriented not to actions but to objects, in that it
prohibits a person from deriving any benefit from an item. The thrust
of a vow prohibits the object ("this item shall be forbidden to me").

Another difference between an oath and a vow concerns the
formula of expression. An oath must employ the word *shevuah* (or
acceptable substitutes), and it must be taken in the name of God (or
acceptable euphemisms). In contrast, vows were frequently made at
sacred sites or taken in the presence of sacred objects.[5] But all these
distinctions established by the rabbis were frequently blurred by the
folk in actual practice.

The making of vows and oaths were common in the everyday
life and ordinary speech of antiquity.[6] Their purpose was to raise one's
credibility and to convince another party that one's statements were
true or that one's promises would be carried out.

People made oaths at home, on the streets, and in business.
Business people would encourage a sale by vowing not to sell below

---

3. Buchanan believes that *korban* and its substitutes literally referred to
a sacred object on which the vow was taken. See George Wesley Buchanan,
"Some Vow and Oath Formulas in the New Testament," *Harvard Theological Review* 58 (July 1965): 320.

4. Rabinovitch, *Tractate Nedarim*, 2; Saul Lieberman, "Oaths and Vows,"
chap. in *Greek in Jewish Palestine* (New York: Jewish Theological Seminary
of America, 1942), 117; Ze'ev Falk, "On Talmudic Vows," *Harvard Theological Review* 59 (July 1966): 309.

5. Buchanan, "Some Vow and Oath Formulas," 323; see Chapter One,
p. 3 n. 3.

6. Lieberman, *Greek*, 115.

or buy above a certain price (M. *Nedarim* 3:1). Big talkers would take a vow in order to persuade their incredulous listeners that the story was true (M. *Nedarim* 3:2). It was a common practice to coerce the attendance of a guest at dinner by means of a vow (M. *Nedarim* 3:1). A vow could be utilized to create a sanction against another party, thereby depriving them of any benefit from one's possessions (M. *Nedarim* 3:3).

The power of the vow or oath to convince the other party did not inhere in the mere promise of sincerity. The credibility of an oath or vow was due to the potential activation of a curse against the vower, should one fail to deliver on the content of one's vow or lie about one's oath. The curse was an integral part of the vow or oath:[7]

> "I make you swear and may it come upon you." "I make you swear" implies the imposition of the oath. "May it come upon you" implies the curse (J. T. *Sotah* 2:1).

and

> All the oaths imposed by the Torah should consist of an oath and a curse (*Sifre* 1:1).

For superstitious reasons many biblical oath formulas omitted or otherwise truncated the curse.[8] The omission of the negative was also common. Many rabbinic vows and oaths lack the curse for the same reason. The prohibitive vows of *Mishnah Nedarim* and *Mishnah Shevuot* fit into this category. *Mishnah Shevuot* 3:4 provides an illustration of truncated formulas:

---

7. Personal communication from Rabbi Manuel Gold; Lieberman, *Greek*, 121; Falk ("On Talmudic Vows," 309–310) denies that vows had anything to do with curses.

8. The curse was certainly an essential part of the biblical oath as well. See Moshe Greenberg, "Oaths," in *Encyclopaedia Judaica*, 1972 ed.

1. *"Konam* (= *Korban*)
2. May my wife benefit from me,
3. If I have eaten today."

Line two is really a curse that has been obscured by the omission of the negative: "May my wife [never] benefit from me." Line
three is the condition under which the curse would be activated.[9] In
some vows the curse has been eliminated altogether:

Konam, if I sell to you for less than a selah (M. *Nedarim* 3:1).

Consequently, the undertaking of a vow or oath implied risk to
oneself, to one's property, or to a loved one. The vower frequently
put his own life at stake with the vow formula, "May such and such
befall me if . . ." or "So and so if I. . . ."[10] Some people swore by the
life of a loved one.[11] As we have just discussed, some people vowed
by placing into jeopardy the benefit they derived from their possessions by the formula, *"Korban* be this item to me."

In this context the biblical and rabbinic statements against
vows and oaths take on a new significance. Deuteronomy 23:23 and
Ecclesiates 5:4 urged people not to make vows. Similarly, we have a
rabbinic proverb: "Right or wrong, do not involve yourself in an
oath."[12] The seriousness with which vows and oaths were held was
due not only to their abstract legal and ethical stature, but also to
the concrete fact that the abuse of a vow or oath activated the curse
the swearer had imposed upon himself or herself, or a loved one.

The *Mishnah* describes the important role of vows and oaths in
everyday life. But except for some clues here and there, the *Mishnah*
conceals the prominent role accorded vows and oaths in the world

---

9. Buchanan, "Some Vow and Oath Formulas," 320–321.
10. Lieberman, *Greek*, 121–123.
11. Ibid., 117.
12. Lieberman, *Greek*, 124 n. 74.

of magic as described in the Babylonian Talmud and exemplified by Babylonian magical incantations.

Both Montgomery and Lieberman have demonstrated that vows and oaths, and the formulae associated with them, operated in two realms—the mundane and the magical.[13] But the magical application of vows and oaths was not limited to the magician. The uttering of oaths and vows in a magical context was also a part of everyday folk religion in antiquity.

It was a popular folk practice to call upon the deities to insure the success or safety of various undertakings by taking an oath in the name of the deity.[14] But the practice of swearing by the name of the deity was not a prayer in the form of an oath; it was an incantation formula, a magical spell, whose purpose was to compel the deity to perform a beneficent act or to make the swearer's words come true.[15] Such incantations are attested in biblical literature:

> Elijah the Tishbite, an inhabitant of Gilead, said to Ahab, "As the LORD lives, the God of Israel whom I serve, there will be no dew or rain except at my bidding" (1 Kings 17:1).

and

---

13. James A. Montgomery, *Aramaic Incantation Texts from Nippur* (Philadelphia: University of Pennsylvania Press, 1913), 51–53; Lieberman, *Greek*, 119–120; idem, "Some Notes on Adjurations in Israel," chap. in *Texts and Studies* (New York: Ktav, 1974), 21–28.

14. In order to avoid using the actual name of God and to lessen the power of the curse, many popular euphemisms were employed to invoke God indirectly. Some vows were sworn by the cosmic objects God had created, such as the sun, stars, the heaven and earth. See Rambam, *Mishneh Torah, Hilkhot Shevuot* 12:3; Lieberman, *Greek*, 124. Others vowed by God's attributes (M. *Shevuot* 4:13). Still others swore by holy objects such as Jerusalem, the Temple, the altar. See Lieberman, *Greek*, 132.

15. Lieberman, "Adjurations in Israel," 24, and "Fears and Pleasures," chap. in *Greek in Jewish Palestine*, 108 n. 85.

They call upon chariots, they call upon horses, but we call on the name of the LORD our God (Psalm 20:8).

The same formulae can be found in rabbinic literature as well:

I swear by Your great name that I will not budge from this spot (M. *Taanit* 3:8).[16]

and

People swear by invoking Him who established the world on three pillars (*Shir haShirim Rabbah* 7:8).

Folk religion constantly blurred the distinction between prayer and incantation, between the liturgical and the magical. These texts demonstrate that the act of swearing by the name of the deity was popularly understood as the invocation of a magic spell. Although these magical practices were examples of therapeutic magic, the rabbis still fought against these incantation formulae and converted them into liturgical prayers whenever they could.[17]

Vows and oaths were also utilized in the process of destructive magic.[18] Believing in the magical power of words in general, the practitioners of destructive magic took over the terminology and formulae for the creation of binding commitments and obligations in the human world and applied them to the satanic realm. Consequently, such terms as *neder*, *issar*, and *shevuah* were synonymous in the

---

16. It was common for a person to bind himself by an oath that involved the action by a deity. Such an oath "puts the squeeze," so to speak, on the deity to perform. Otherwise the deity causes the person to have perjured oneself! See Lieberman, "Pleasures and Fears," in *Greek*, 108 n. 85.

17. Lieberman, "Adjurations in Israel," 24.

18. I avoid using the conventional terms "white magic" or "black magic" due to their implicit racism.

Babylonian incantation texts with curses and other types of hostile spells engendered by destructive magic:[19]

> Appointed is this bowl for the sealing and guarding of the house and sons and property and body of Maiducht, daughter of Kumboi, that she may be guarded from demons, plagues, devil, satans, seducers, diaboli, and from any vows [nidra], invocations, and rites of humankind.[20]

and

> Wholly charmed and sealed and bound and enchanted [are you], that you go away and be sealed and depart from the house [and property?] of Farruch bar Pusbi and Newanduch, daughter of Pusbi and Abanduch, daughter of Pusbi, and that there depart from them all evil liliths and all demons, and devils, spells, idol-spirits, and the vow [nidra], the curse, and the invocation, and evil arts and mighty works and everything hostile.[21]

The Babylonian Talmud was clearly aware of this usage as well. In *Sanhedrin* 68a Rabbi Joshua exclaims: "The ban [neder] is lifted."

Consequently, vows were not to be toyed with. They were a powerful weapon that could be manipulated by human beings to help or hurt other human beings. The individual needed protection not only from curses that were activated by his own abused vows, but also from malevolent vows, that is, curses, which had been directed by destructive magic against his or her person.

---

19. Montgomery, *Aramaic Incantation Texts*, 52, 84; Lieberman, *Greek*, 119.

20. Montgomery, *Aramaic Incantation Texts*, 236; this incantation is also cited by Jacob Neusner, *A History of the Jews in Babylonia*, vol. 6 (Leiden: E. J. Brill, 1970), 225–226.

21. Montgomery, *Aramaic Incantation Texts*, 138.

In Chapter One, the religious dimension of vows in the Bible was demonstrated. Now the prominent role accorded vows in social affairs and the world of magic as well has come to light. In contrast to the strictly religious character of vows presented in the Hebrew Bible, by rabbinic times, vows also functioned to persuade or coerce in the social sphere and to conjure therapeutic or destructive magic. Folk religion constantly blurred the rabbis' legal distinctions between vows and oaths, between self-imposed obligations to God and solemn promises to others.

Yet the significance of vows in antiquity cannot be fully appreciated until the relationship between vows and demons, and the critical role played by vows in incantations, are further elucidated.

3

The Nullification of Vows in the *Mishnah* and the *Talmudim*

Despite the absence of a biblical precedent for the nullification of vows, a procedure to annul vows does exist in rabbinic tradition. The absence of biblical support for the practice was candidly acknowledged in *Mishnah Chagigah* 1:8:

> [The rules about] release from vows [by a sage] hover in the air and have nothing to support them.[1]

However, several biblical proof-texts were adduced in *Chagigah* 10a to demonstrate that the nullification of vows was biblically based. The rules of *hatarat nedarim* are complex. For the purposes of our study, these are the most salient points:

1. An individual cannot annul one's own vow (M. *Negaim* 2:5). Only a sage has the authority to annul a vow (B. T. *Shevuot*

---

1. Maimonides wrote (*Mishneh Torah, Sefer Haflaah, Hilkhot Shevuot* 6:2): "[The absolution from oaths] has no basis whatsoever in the Written Torah."

19

28a). In the absence of a sage, however, a vow can be nullified by three knowledgeable laymen, that is, a *bet din* (M. *Nedarim* 2:5; B. T. *Bekorot* 36b/37a).[2]

2. The vower must specify the contents of the vow to the sage or the *bet din* (B. T. *Gittin* 35b).

The grounds for the nullification of vows in Jewish law are based upon the concept of "regret" (*charatah*). *Charatah* has two possible forms, one simple and one complex. Simple "regret" occurs when an individual expresses sincere regret for his vow and claims that it was made under abnormal circumstances, such as in a fit of rage (B. T. *Nedarim* 21a/22b).[3] Under some circumstances this may be sufficient grounds to annul a vow.

But in Jewish law the mere fact that an individual regrets having undertaken a vow does not, in most instances, release the person from the vow. Most often the second and more complex form of *charatah* is required. In this instance the sage or *bet din* must find a *petach charatah* (opening of regret) for the vower. A *petach* is a forseeable but unconsidered fact, circumstance, or consequence, such that the vower can truthfully claim, "Had I known or considered X, I would not have made this vow" (M. *Nedarim* 2:1,5; chap. 9 and B. T. *Nedarim* 22b, 77b).[4]

Maimonides (Rambam) described the procedure for the nullification of vows in the following manner:

---

2. Rambam, *Mishneh Torah, Sefer Haflaah, Hilkhot Nedarim* 4:5 and *Hilkhot Shevuot* 6:1.

3. *Encyclopedia Talmudit*, 2nd rev. ed. (1973), s.v. "*Hatarat Nedarim*"; Rabinovitch, *Tractate Nedarim*, 28.

4. *Encyclopedia Talmudit*, 2nd rev. ed. (1973), s.v. "*Hatarat Nedarim*"; Rabinovitch, *Tractate Nedarim*, 28, 162–163; Louis Isaac Rabinowitz, "Vows and Vowing," in *Encyclopaedia Judaica*, 1972 ed.; Ze'ev W. Falk, "Binding and Loosing," in *Studies in Jewish Legal History: Essays in Honour of David Daube*, ed. Bernard S. Jackson (London: Jewish Chronicle Publications, 1974), 97.

The swearer must appear before an outstanding scholar or before three ordinary men where no expert is available and say, 'I swore an oath concerning such and such matter, and I now regret it. Had I known that I would be in such distress through it, or that such and such a thing would happen to me, I would not have sworn,' or 'had I been of the same mind at the time of swearing as I am now, I would not have sworn.' The sage, or the senior of the three consultants, should then say to him, 'and do you indeed regret it?' He should reply, 'yes.' Whereupon the sage should say to him, 'you are released' [sharui lekha] or 'you are absolved' [mutar lekha] or 'you are pardoned' [machol lekha] or something to the same effect in any language.[5]

The annulment was justified on the grounds that since the vower neglected to realize all the ramifications of his vow, he made the vow by mistake. The sage or bet din annulled the vow on the basis that it was not the vower's true intent to undertake this vow. But if the vower was lying about his feelings of regret, then the vow remained binding even if the sage or bet din annulled it. In modern parlance, we would designate the process of potchim petach as "finding a legal loophole."[6] Indeed, Ze'ev Falk cites this procedure as an example of legal fiction in Jewish law.[7]

The feasibility of various reasons as potential petachim are discussed in Mishnah Nedarim, chapter 9.[8] Among the reasons considered to be acceptable as a petach charatah are: the motive for the vow has been eliminated (9:3); the vow conflicts with a biblical commandment (9:4); the vow conflicts with a Shabbat or festival requirement (9:6); there is a question of the honor of self or children (9:9); a vow is based on false assumptions or misinformation (9:10). Rejected as

---

5. Rambam, Mishneh Torah, Sefer Haflaah, Hilkhot Shavuot 6:5.

6. See M. Nedarim 2:1; chap. 9 (all).

7. Ze'ev W. Falk, Introduction to Jewish Law of the Second Commonwealth (Leiden: E. J. Brill, 1972), 23.

8. See Rabinovitch's discussion (Tractate Nedarim, 162–183).

acceptable reasons were parental dignity (9:1) and unexpected consequences (9:2). Subsequently, it was ruled in *Nedarim* 21b that four
categories of vows (as cited by the rabbis in *Mishnah Nedarim* 3:1)
were not binding: vows made to induce bargaining, vows of exaggera-
tion, vows made under false assumptions or facts, and vows that cannot be fulfilled due to some compelling and unavoidable circumstance.[9]

As adumbrated in Chapter One, both the *Mishnah* and the Talmud made a strong theoretical and legal distinction between *hatarat
nedarim* and *hafarat nedarim*. This distinction was reflected in the
careful and consistent practice throughout *Mishnah Nedarim* of em-
ploying the term *hafarah* in regard to the nullification of women's vows
and the term *hatarah* for all others.

This differentiation practiced by *Mishnah Nedarim* was explicitly expressed by the Rambam in his description of what the sage can
and cannot say at the conclusion of the procedure for the nullification of vows:

> Whereupon the sage should say to him, 'you are released' [*sharui
> lekha*] or 'you are absolved' [*mutar lekha*] or 'you are pardoned'
> [*machol lekha*]. But if he says to him 'it's now revoked for you'
> [*mufar lekha*] or 'your oath is eradicated' [*ne'ekra shevuatcha*] or
> anything with a similar meaning, his words are of no effect. For

---

9. In this connection it's important to point out that the frequently negative aphorisms regarding vows in the Talmud have been misunderstood. For
example: Samuel said "even when one fulfills his vow, he is called wicked"
(B. T. *Nedarim* 22a, 77b); it's claimed in B. T. *Shabbat* 32b that children
die prematurely as a result of their parents' vows; R. Nathan said, "One who
vows is as though he built a high place [for idolatry], and he who fulfills it
is as though he sacrificed on it (B. T. *Nedarim* 22a). These statements were
not merely *aggadah*. Originally they functioned as potential *petachim*! That
is, a sage might ask a vower in search of absolution, "Would you have vowed
had you known that it's wicked to do so?" and so on. See B. T. *Nedarim*
21b.

only a husband or a father can revoke an oath; a sage may speak only in terms of absolution [*hatarah*] or pardon [*mechilah*].[10]

Neither the sage nor the *bet din* possessed the authority to revoke a vow that had already been uttered. Instead, they resorted to a legal fiction by which they retroactively annulled the vow *ab initio*, at the moment of its inception. By means of such a legal fiction it could be argued that the vow had not been revoked. Rather, it was as if the vow did not exist and had never existed:[11]

The sage loosens and uproots the vow from its very root.[12]

Thus, the sage could say:

There is no vow here, there is no oath here (P. T. *Nedarim* 10:8).

The Rambam ruled in the passage cited above that the phrase *mutar lekha* or its synonyms need be said only once. There was, however, an earlier talmudic tradition that the nullification of vows must be declared three times (B. T. *Menachot* 65a). Later *poskim* adopted this opinion and ruled in addition that only the term *mutar lekha* should be utilized.[13]

Up to this point we have been discussing the retroactive annulment of vows where the vows have already been uttered and conse-

---

10. Rambam, *Mishneh Torah, Sefer Haflaah, Hilkhot Shevuot* 6:5.

11. Albeck, *Shishah Sidrei Mishnah, Seder Nashim, Masekhet Nedarim*, 141; Rabinovitch, *Tractate Nedarim*, 184; *Encyclopedia Talmudit*, 2nd rev. ed. (1974), s.v. "*Hatarat Nedarim*."

12. B. T. *Ketubot* 74b; P. T. *Ketubot* 7:7. Both sources contrast the power of a doctor to cure an illness with the power of a sage to annul a vow. The doctor can heal an illness only from the time he applies medicine. He cannot retroactively cure the illness. But the sage can uproot a vow from its roots, as if it had never taken effect and never existed.

13. B. T. *Shabbat* 68a; *Bet Yosef* to *Tur, Yoreh De'ah* 228.

quently considered in force. Jewish law also recognizes a procedure
for the anticipatory invalidation of vows that may be undertaken in
the future. This procedure involves the declaration of intent to invalidate future vows in the form of an advance stipulation (*bitul tenai*).

The *locus classicus* for the anticipatory invalidation of future vows
is B. T. *Nedarim* 23b. The *mishnah* under discussion in this *gemara* is
Mishnah Nedarim 3:1:

> He who desires that none of his vows made during the year shall
> be valid, let him stand at Rosh haShanah and declare, "Every
> vow which I may make in the future shall be cancelled," pro-
> vided that he remembers [the stipulation] at the time of the vow.

While the nullification of vows *ab initio* allows people to annul
vows already in force, this procedure prevents vows from ever taking
force. Placed in the general context of *Mishnah Nedarim*, which refers
to prohibitive vows (*nidrei issur*), this practice pertains solely to prohibitive vows, that is, where the vower abstains from eating, drink-
ing, or the like.[14]

There is a debate in the *Gemara* between Rava and Abbaye in
which they question the logic of why a vow would need to be cancelled since the vower remembers his or her original stipulation.
Abbaye argues that logic required the opposite conclusion. For if the
vower makes a vow with complete remembrance of his or her original stipulation, then it must have been the person's intent to undertake the vow and overrule the prior stipulation. Abbaye proposes that
the *mishnah* should be emended to read "provided it is not remem-
bered at the time of the vow." Wanting to avoid an emendation of
the text, Rava maintains that the *mishnah* is correct as given. To prove
his point, Rava constructs a hypothetical case in which the given
mishnah makes perfect sense.

---

14. See Rosh to *Nedarim* 23b.

The details of the arguments Rava and Abbaye put forth are not germane to our study.[15] The salient point for our purpose is that later commentators harmonized the views of Rava and Abbaye, arguing that Abbaye and Rava differed only because they were addressing different cases. This allowed later authorities to adopt Abbaye's opinion as the law: if the vower remembers his or her declaration of invalidation, then the vow is binding—but to base it on Rava's greater authority.[16]

Most significantly, Rava ruled that this procedure for the anticipatory invalidation of future vows should not be taught to the public. He feared that it would lead the general population to disregard their vows and to take them lightly:

> R. Huna b. Hinena wished to lecture [on the invalidation of future vows] publicly. But Rava remonstrated with him. The

---

15. Abbaye reasoned in the following manner: An individual declared a general invalidation of future vows. If the person went ahead and made a vow, with full remembrance of his original stipulation, then it must have been the individual's current intent to supersede his prior stipulation and undertake the vow. Conversely, if the person undertook a vow but did not remember that he had made a prior stipulation, then his present intent is not clear. Without any definitive statement to the contrary, the original stipulation remains in force, and the vow has no legal effect.

Rava reasoned in the following manner: An individual declared specific future vows to be invalid. The person went ahead and made a vow, with full remembrance that he had made a stipulation but having forgotten the specifics. If the individual declared that he wished the vow to be considered as part of his original stipulation, then the vower's present intent is quite clear, and the vow is cancelled. Conversely, if the vower did not make this declaration, then the vower's current intent must have been to undertake the vow and override his prior stipulation.

16. Rambam, *Mishheh Torah, Sefer Haflaah, Hilkhot Nedarim* 2:4,5; *Shulchan Arukh, Yoreh De'ah* 211:2.

Tanna has intentionally obscured the law in order that vows should not be treated lightly, but you desire to teach it publicly!

Rava's misgivings notwithstanding, B. T. *Nedarim* 23b became the authority for a popular practice in the Middle Ages of nullifying both past and future vows on the morning before Rosh haShanah:

> Pious Jews still follow a procedure based on this original practice: after the morning worship on the day preceding Rosh haShanah, they petition a 'court' of three learned men to hear declarations pertaining both to vows unwittingly neglected during the past year and those which might be improperly taken during the year about to begin.[17]

But for our study, *Nedarim* 23b holds even greater historical significance. By the eighth century, some Geonic *responsa* report that *Nedarim* 23b was attributed to be the talmudic authority for another highly popular folk practice—*kol nidrei*. In the next chapter it will be shown that the terminology of *kol nidrei* proves it is a retroactive nullification of vows *ab initio*.

---

17. Herman Kieval, "The Curious Case of Kol Nidre," *Commentary* 46 (October 1968): 53.

II
THE *KOL NIDREI* FORMULA

4

Versions of *Kol Nidrei*

The author of *kol nidrei* and its exact date of origin are unknown. The earliest known version of *kol nidrei* is recorded in the ninth-century prayer book *Seder Rav Amram*. The text is mostly in Hebrew:

> All *nedarim, isarim, shevuot, kiyumim* and *charamim*,[1] which we have vowed, imposed, declared, sworn, and obligated upon ourselves under oath[2] from the previous Day of Atonement until this Day of Atonement which has come to us,[3] we retract all of them and we come before our Father in heaven [to say]. If we

---

1. "Vows, prohibitive vows, oaths, contracts, and vows of dedication." *Charamim*: a special declaration consecrating something to the Temple or to the priests (M. *Nedarim* 1:1). See the discussion in Chapter Two, pp. 11–12.

2. *Beshavuah*: perhaps it connotes the meaning "under law."

3. This is the conventional translation of *haba aleinu*. But several factors call its veracity to question. First of all, the phrase is redundant. The apposition between the previous Day of Atonement and the present Day of Atonement is made perfectly clear by the demonstrative *zeh*. Note too that *zeh* appears in Hai Gaon's *kol nidrei* but *haba aleinu* does not. Secondly, the term *lavo aleinu* means in 2 Samuel 17:2 "to set upon, to attack." Perhaps *haba aleinu* is an allusion to Yom Kippur as a day of judgment, particularly in light of the later phrase, "may it come upon us for good."

uttered a *neder*, now there is no *neder*. If we bound ourselves by an *isar*, now there is no *isar*. If we declared a *cherem*, now there is no *cherem*. If we took a *shevuah*, now there is no *shevuah*. If we made a *kiyum*, now there is no *kiyum*. Annul the *neder* from its root. Annul the *isar* from its root. Annul the *cherem* from its root. Annul the *kiyum* from its root. Now there is no *neder*, no *isar*, no *shevuah*, and no *kiyum*. Now there is pardon, forgiveness, and atonement as it is written in Your Torah, 'The whole Israelite community and the stranger residing among them shall be forgiven, for the entire people acted in error' (Numbers 15:26).[4]

Amram's *kol nidrei* begins with a listing of five different types of vows that were undertaken between the previous Day of Atonement and the present one. The key point here is that all these vows have been uttered. Consequently, they are already in force.

From the talmudic sources cited in Chapter Three, we can now recognize that Amram's *kol nidrei* extensively borrows from the legal terminology and conceptual ideas for the nullification of vows (*hatarat nedarim*). By the retroactive nullification of the vows from their root (*batel haneder me'ikaro*), that is, from the very moment they took force, *kol nidrei* renders the vows as if they no longer exist and had never existed.[5] By means of this legal fiction, the *kol nidrei* formula properly asserts "Now there is no vow" (*ein kan neder*).[6] Thus we con-

---

4. Daniel Goldschmidt, ed., *Seder Rav Amram Gaon* (Jerusalem: Mossad haRav Kook, 1971), 162. The Karaite Sahl ben Masliah reported the existence of an abbreviated *kol nidrei* form in the ninth century: "All *nedarim, shavuot, issarim, kiyumim* which we have vowed, sworn, imposed and obligated from the fast of the previous Day of Atonement to this fast of the Day of Atonement. All of them are forgiven, annulled, pardoned." See Jacob Mann, *Texts and Studies* (Cincinnati: Hebrew Union College Press, 1931), 51;88.

5. "The sage loosens and uproots the vow." See B. T. *Ketubot* 74b and P. T. *Ketubot* 7:7. See our discussion in Chapter Three, p. 23.

6. The sage says, "There is no vow here, there is no oath here" (P. T. *Nedarim* 10:8). See our discussion in Chapter Three, p. 23.

clude that *kol nidrei* constitutes a retroactive nullification of vows *ab initio.*

Another version of *kol nidrei* was composed by Hai Gaon. Since there are two *Geonim* named Hai Gaon, the authorship of this *kol nidrei* is a matter of debate. Goldschmidt and Deshen attribute this *kol nidrei* to Hai bar Nachshon (of Sura, 871–879).[7] But Mann and Kieval attribute this *kol nidrei* to Hai bar Sherira (of Pumbedita, 998–1038).[8] Since Hai bar Nachshon fervently opposed the practice of *kol nidrei*, it doesn't seem likely that he would compose and promulgate a new version.[9] Given that no known criticisms of *kol nidrei* have been attributed to Hai bar Sherira, it is reasonable to attribute this *kol nidrei* version to Hai bar Sherira Gaon.

We know the text of Hai Gaon's *kol nidrei* through a citation found in *Shibbolei haLeket*, composed by the thirteenth-century Italian *posek* Zedekiah ben Abraham:[10]

> All *nidrei, isarei, konamei, charamei,* and *shevuei*[11] which we have vowed, sworn, declared, and imposed upon ourselves from the previous Day of the Fast of Atonement until this Day of the Fast of Atonement upon which we have transgressed inadvertently or by compelling circumstances, we pray for compassion from the Lord of heaven to release us and to forgive us. Our *nidrei* are not

---

7. Daniel Goldschmidt, *Machzor laYamim haNoraim*, vol. 1 (New York: Leo Baeck Institute, 1970), 27; Deshen, "The Enigma of *Kol Nidre*," 147 n. 17.

8. Mann, *Texts and Studies*, 52 n. 27; Deshen, "The Enigma of *Kol Nidre*," 147 n. 17.

9. See the discussion in Chapter Eight.

10. *Shibbolei haLeket*, ed. Solomon Buber (Jerusalem, 1962), *Seder Yom haKippurim* #317.

11. "All vows, prohibitive vows, *konam*-vows, vows of dedication, and oaths. . . ." *Konamei:* a class of vows that used *konam* as an acceptable substitute for *korban* in the vow formula, "This is forbidden to me like a *korban*" or "*Korban* be this item to me." See the discussion in Chapter Two, pp. 11–12.

nidrei to be liable for them; our *isarei* are not *isarei* to sin by them; and our *shevuei* are not *shevuei* to be punished on account of them, as it is written "they shall be forgiven. . . ."

The version of *kol nidrei* known to Rav Amram was mostly in Hebrew. Hai Gaon's *kol nidrei* was a conflation of Palestinian and Babylonian Aramaic. Aside from this the two *kol nidrei* versions share some basic similarities. Both versions list five types of vows, of which four are the same. The exception is that Amram's text used *kiyum*, while Hai's version employed *konamei*. Both texts refer to past vows. Both sources invoke Numbers 15:26 as proof-text.

But a close analysis of the different terminologies employed by these *kol nidrei* texts illuminate some striking differences in substantive content. Goldschmidt maintains that *kol nidrei*'s affinity with *hatarat nedarim* was purely superficial. He argues that the failure of the *kol nidrei* text preserved by Rav Amram to fulfill the talmudic requirements for the nullification of vows demonstrates that it was intended for a different purpose. Goldschmidt claims that the content of *kol nidrei* reveals its true function:

> [*Kol nidrei*] is a petition for compassion so that the vows to which they had obligated themselves are not operative and they desired by this to be saved from punishment.[12]

Contrary to Goldschmidt, however, the very language of Amram's *kol nidrei* formula, which was analyzed earlier in this chapter, proves that it was intended as a nullification of vows. Moreover, Goldschmidt vitiated his own argument by stating that Hai Gaon's *kol nidrei* rescued the practice from rabbinic opposition.[13] If Amram's version of *kol nidrei* were truly a prayer for absolution, why were some of the *Geonim* opposed to it? If this version of *kol nidrei* was simply a prayer for absolution, then why was Hai's version preferable?

---

12. Goldschmidt, *Machzor*, 26.
13. Ibid., 27

Goldschmidt's hypothesis far more accurately describes Hai Gaon's *kol nidrei*.[14] Here the linguistic terminology for *hatarat nedarim* is noticeably absent. There is no mention of "annulling the vow from its root" or "now there is no vow." Quite the contrary, this version of *kol nidrei* is permeated with the language of penitential prayer:

> We pray for compassion from the Lord of heaven to release us and to forgive us.

The prayer's concern to escape divine punishment is paramount:

> Our vows are not vows to be liable for them; our prohibitive vows are not prohibitive vows to sin by them; and our oaths are not oaths to be punished on account of them. . . .

In this regard, two other differences between the *kol nidrei* versions are worthy of note. The *kol nidrei* known to Rav Amram provided a blanket nullification of vows, even if the vows were intentionally violated. But Hai Gaon's *kol nidrei* limited the release to only those vows that went unfulfilled due to unintentional neglect or compelling circumstances. Second, God appears to play almost no active role in Rav Amram's *kol nidrei*. The people ascribe to themselves the authority to nullify their vows. God's pardon and forgiveness are invoked at the end. In contrast, quite explicit in Hai Gaon's *kol nidrei* is the notion that it is up to God to forgive the people and to release them from their vows.

It is most probable, then, that the *kol nidrei* version extant in *Seder Rav Amram* functioned as a genuine nullification of vows. By contrast, Hai Gaon's *kol nidrei* was not a *hatarat nedarim*, but a prayer for absolution.[15] In Chapter Eight the attitude of the Babylonian

---

14. Deshen ("The Enigma of *Kol Nidre*," 147 n. 17) agrees with this estimation: "Hai bar Nachshon (sic) more suitably revises the custom as a request for pardon from the transgression of vows."

15. Lieberman maintains that the rabbis fought against incantational formulae and tried to convert them into liturgical prayers whenever they

Geonim toward *kol nidrei* will be discussed in greater detail. Let it suffice for now to say that these distinctions between the two *kol nidrei* versions may have played an important role in their deliberations.

Abramson has shown that *kol nidrei* was once accompanied by a blessing for the nullification of vows.[16] The blessing is in Hebrew:

> Praised are You, Adonai our God, King of the universe, who sanctified us with commandments and commanded us concerning the nullification of vows and oaths.

Abramson found the blessing at the end of the *kol nidrei* text recorded in a book called *The Book of Apples* (*Kittab al Tapatha*), which he claims was written in Egypt during the late eleventh/early twelfth century. But the Karaite Salman ben Yerucham was already aware of the blessing in the second half of the ninth century.[17] *Shibbolei haLeket* mentions that the blessing was still being practiced as late as the thirteenth century.[18]

Believing that *kol nidrei* failed to meet any of the necessary talmudic requirements for the nullification of past vows, Rabbenu Tam changed *kol nidrei* in the twelfth century to refer to future vows and added a reference to the principle of *charatah*.[19] He converted the phrase "from the previous Day of Atonement to this Day of Atonement" to:

> From this Day of Atonement until the next Day of Atonement may it come upon us for good. Regarding them all, we regret (*etcharatna*) them.

---

could. Hai's *kol nidrei* may be a good example of that process. See Lieberman, "Adjurations in Israel," 24–25.

16. Shraga Abramson, "Early Rulings," [Hebrew] *Sinai* 49 (1961): 210–214; "On the Blessing for the Nullification of Vows and Oaths," [Hebrew] *Sinai* 50 (1962): 185–186.

17. Mann, *Texts and Studies*, 51, 85.

18. *Shibbolei haLeket, Seder Yom haKippurim* #317.

19. See the detailed discussion in Chapter Nine.

This emendation was not widely accepted among *Ashkenazim* until the seventeenth century. It was never accepted among Western *Sephardim* (Spain and Portugal). Oriental *Sephardim* incorporated both phrases within the *kol nidrei* formula.[20] An analysis of all three *kol nidrei* versions follows.[21]

Below is the classical *Ashkenazi kol nidrei*:[22]

All *nidrei, esarei, charamei, konamei, chinuyei, kinusei,* and *shevuei*[23] which we have vowed, sworn, declared, and imposed upon ourselves from this Day of Atonement until the next Day of Atonement may it come upon us for good. Regarding them all, we regret them. Let them all be released,[24] forgiven,[25] erased,[26] null and void.[27] They are not valid nor are they in force.[28] Our vows [*nidreina*] are not vows. Our prohibitive vows [*esareina*] are not prohibitive vows. Our oaths [*shevu'atana*] are not oaths.

---

20. Kieval, "The Curious Case of *Kol Nidre*," 55.

21. The Aramaic texts can be found in Appendix I.

22. As cited in Goldschmidt, *Machzor,* 2.

23. "All vows, prohibitive vows, oaths, vows of dedication, *konam-*vows, *konas-*vows, and equivalent terms. . . ." *Kinusei*: a class of vows that use *konas* as an acceptable substitute for *korban* in the vow formula; *chinuyei*: the entire class of all terms considered acceptable euphemisms for *korban* in the vow formula.

24. *Shiran*: similar to *mutar lekha,* "You are released." Others translate as "permitted."

25. *Shevikin*: similar to *machul lekha,* "You are forgiven, pardoned." In other contexts it can also connote "to abandon, to leave," but it is erroneous to so translate here.

26. *Shevitin*: the term does not occur elsewhere in rabbinic literature. Goldschmidt identified it as "erased," synonymous with *machui* and *machuk.*

27. *Betalin umevutalin*: generally rendered "cancelled." But this misses the phrase's force as a synonym for "nullification." Hence the closest English equivalent is "null and void."

28. *La sheririn vela kayamin*: the positive form *sharir v'kayam* is the customary formula appearing at the end of a document and certifies it as valid and in force—and consequently enforceable!

From a purely linguistic point of view this classical *Ashkenazi kol nidrei* is much closer to Hai Gaon's *kol nidrei*: (1) it is written in Aramaic; (2) it lists all five types of vows mentioned by Hai Gaon; (3) it employs the same verbs in the same order ("which we have vowed, sworn, declared, and imposed ourselves"); finally, (4) like Hai Gaon's *kol nidrei*, the classic *kol nidrei* employs the terms *sherei* (release) and *shevak* (forgive).

But the classic *Ashkenazi kol nidrei* does not utilize the language of penitential prayer exclusively. We also find some terminology associated with the nullification of vows such as *charatah* and *betalin umevutalin*, though only the root *batel* is represented from *Seder Rav Amram*. Instead we have new terms such as *shevitin* and *la sheririn vela kayamin*.

The classical Western Sephardi formulation of *kol nidrei* is:[29]

The rabbi says:

All *nidrei, esarei, shevuei, charamei, niduyei, kunamei, kunachei,* and *kunasei*[30] which we have vowed, sworn, declared, pronounced, and imposed upon ourselves from the previous Yom Kippur until this Yom Kippur which has come upon us in peace.

Congregation responds:

Our vows (*nidreina*) are not vows. Our oaths (*shevu'ana*) are not oaths. Our vows of dedication (*charamana*) are not vows of dedication. Our excommunications (*niduyana*) are not excommunications. Our prohibitive vows (*esarana*) are not prohibitive vows.

---

29. David de Sola Pool, ed. *Prayers for the Day of Atonement: According to the Custom of the Spanish and Portuguese Jews* (New York: Union of Sephardic Congregations, 1984), 26.

30. "All vows, prohibitive vows, oaths, vows of dedication, excommunications, *konam*-vows, *konach*-vows, *konas*-vows. . . ." *Niduyei*: excommunications; *kunachei*: a set of vows that use *konach* as an acceptable substitute for *korban* in the vow formula; *kunasei*: another form of *kinusei*.

Regarding them all, let them be erased and forgiven. They are not valid nor are they in force. "The whole Israelite community and the stranger residing among them shall be forgiven, for the entire people acted in error" (Numbers 15:26).

The traditional Western Sephardi *kol nidrei* also follows the linguistic patterns of Hai Gaon's *kol nidrei*: (1) it is written in Aramaic; (2) it lists all five types of vows mentioned by Hai Gaon; (3) with one exception (*nadeina*), it employs the same verbs in the same order; finally, (4) the Sephardi *kol nidrei* employs the term *shevak*.

The Western Sephardi *kol nidrei* shares many linguistic elements with its Ashkenazi counterpart as well. With two exceptions, it lists the same types of vows: The Sephardic text adds *niduyei* and replaces *chinuyei* with *kunachei*. It also shares with the Ashkenazi *kol nidrei* some of the same terminology for the nullification of vows: "They shall be erased and forgiven. They are not valid nor are they in force" (*Yehon shevitin ushevikin. La sharirin vela kayamin*).

But the most glaring difference between the Ashkenazi and Sephardi *kol nidrei* is that the latter does not include Rabbenu Tam's emendation. It refers to past vows. It makes no reference to the principle of *charatah*. The Sephardi version includes Numbers 15:26 within the *kol nidrei* formula. It is chanted antiphonally.

The classic Oriental Sephardic *kol nidrei* formula is:[31]

All *nidrei, esarei, shevuei, niduyei, charamei, kunamei, kunachei, kunasei*, which we have vowed and will vow, sworn and will swear, pronounced and will pronounce, declared and will declare, which we have imposed upon ourselves from the previous Day of Atonement until this Day of Atonement which has come to us in peace, and from this Day of Atonement until the next Day of Atonement, may it come to us in peace. Our vows (*nidrana*) are not vows. Our oaths (*shevu'ana*) are not oaths. Our excom-

---

31. Moshe Rabi, ed. *Machzor Tefillah LeMoshe: Lefi Minhag haSefaradim ve'dot haMizrach* (Jerusalem, 1982), 93–94.

munications (*niduyana*) are not excommunications. Our vows of dedication (*charamana*) are not vows of dedication. Our prohibitive vows (*esarana*) are not prohibitive vows. Regarding them all, we regret them. May it be God's will that they shall be erased and forgiven. They are not valid nor are they in force. "The whole Israelite community and the stranger residing among them shall be forgiven, for the entire people acted in error" (Numbers 15:26).

With two exceptions, the Oriental Sephardi *kol nidrei* and its Western Sephardi counterpart are essentially the same. The obvious difference is that the former has adopted Rabbenu Tam's emendation. It also mentions God. In contrast with the Ashkenazi *kol nidrei*, the Oriental Sephardi version refers to *both* past and future vows. In order to make *kol nidrei* more coherent, the Oriental *kol nidrei*, unlike its Ashkenazi counterpart, lists the verbs in the opening phrase in both the past and future tenses.

Having accepted Rabbenu Tam's emendation, the Oriental Sephardi *kol nidrei* also includes the reference to *charatah*. Otherwise, both Sephardi versions include the same terminology for the nullification of vows. Like Hai Gaon's *kol nidrei*, the Oriental Sephardi *kol nidrei* also uses the term *shevak* (forgive).

All three *kol nidrei* versions straddle the fence between Amram's nullification of vows and Hai's prayer for absolution, by combining both elements in equal measure. For example, both the classic Ashkenazi and Western Sephardi *kol nidrei* lack one element necessary for a prayer of absolution: they never mention God! On the other hand, both the Western and Oriental versions of *kol nidrei* lack a critical element associated with the nullification of vows: they never declare the vows "null and void" (*betalin umevutalin*).

By the thirteenth century *kol nidrei* had undergone another major emendation. In an attempt to further strengthen the legitimacy of *kol nidrei* to nullify past vows, Meir ben Baruch of Rothenberg (Maharam) added a preamble that justified the release from vows on the basis of the consent of the majority.[32] This emendation was universally accepted throughout the Jewish world:

> By authority of the heavenly court and by the authority of this court on earth, with the consent of God and with the consent of this congregation, we permit prayer with transgressors.

For reasons we will explore in Chapter Nine, to the Maharam was also attributed the exclusion of the phrase "As it is written in the Torah of Moses Your servant" from the *kol nidrei* formula.

Finally, it became customary in the late sixteenth/early seventeenth century to recite after the recitation of *kol nidrei*, in addition to Numbers 15:26, two other biblical verses, Numbers 14:19–20:[33]

> The whole Israelite community and the stranger residing among them shall be forgiven for the entire people acted in error (Numbers 15:26).

> Please pardon the sin of this people according to Your great kindness as You have forgiven this people ever since Egypt (Numbers 14:19).

> Then the LORD said, "I pardon as you have asked." (Numbers 14:20).

---

32. See our detailed discussion in Chapter Nine.

33. This dating was conveyed to me in a personal communication from Dr. Menachem Schmelzer.

5

Vows, Demons, and Incantations

The ancients conceived of the world as filled with supernatural beings: gods, angels, demons, and spirits—all presided over by God. Some demons were beneficent and revealed to human beings the decrees of heaven. Others were merely mischievous, but most were malevolent. Thousands of demons inhabited the air, palm trees, house roofs, and privies, and were primary causes of both major disasters and daily inconveniences.

We moderns tend to think of words such as *blessing, curse, vow,* and *oath* in metaphoric terms. The sense that words once uttered have a life of their own and cannot be taken back is explained psychologically by our culture. But the ancients believed that the spoken word took on a metaphysical reality independent of human control.[1] Vows, curses, blessings, and oaths attracted demons and other supernatural beings to carry out the content of the human utterance. Having

---

1. N. H. Snaith, *Leviticus and Numbers,* 321. The impure thoughts of the dying also create demons who may harm the deceased on his journey to heaven or someone else. See Kaufman Kohler, "Demonology," in *The Jewish Encyclopedia,* 1916 ed.

set demons in motion, rash words could not be taken back.[2] This is the context underlying the talmudic warning, "One should never open his mouth to Satan" (B. T. *Berachot* 19a).

It was commonly accepted in antiquity that it was not God or the deities, but demons, who implemented the self-imposed curses activated by abused vows or oaths. An unpublished incantation cited by Shlomo Deshen sheds significant light on the relationship between vows and oaths and the unleashing of demonic forces.[3] This undated manuscript describes the Yom Kippur eve practice in Cheven, a city on the Arabian peninsula near Yemen. The service concludes with an incantation releasing the demons from all the oaths that had been imposed upon them:

> By the authority of the Heavenly Court and by the authority of the Earthly Court, with the consent of the Holy One, blessed be He, and with the consent of Elijah and with the consent of the Rabbinic Court of Jerusalem and with the consent of all the Holy Communities, wherever they are located, we release and annul and cancel all the oaths that have been sworn . . . sworn by every angel and demon and all the angels of destruction and demonic winds against Israel and condemning them from above and by all the generations of Aza and Azael and the forces of Sammael and the generations of Egrat, the daughter of Machalat and Na'ama, the daughter of Tubal-Cain, the wife of Shomron, who is the mother of Ashmodi. Everything shall be released and blotted out and pardon and permission for each oath and spell and charm and talisman and accusation and transformation and euphemism that they have been made to swear to hurt Israel, so that they will not be able to hurt or to accuse or to lead astray

---

2. Joshua Trachtenberg, *Jewish Magic and Superstition: A Study in Folk Religion* (New York: Atheneum, 1939), 44–60.

3. Shlomo Deshen, "The Enigma of 'Kol Nidre': An Anthropological and Historical Approach," [Hebrew], in *Studies in the History of Jewish Society in the Middle Ages and in the Modern Period: Presented to Professor Jacob Katz* (Jerusalem: Magnes Press, 1980), 146.

or to pervert, not from above and not from below, whether by the winds of storm and hurricane, or whether by *gilgul* or whether by foundation or whether by the mixing of combinations, whether by speech or thought, whether by male or female, whether they belong to the Covenant or do not, everything shall be permitted and blotted out and pardon and permission.

This text suggests that when a person undertook an oath or vow, or a magician conjured up a curse, it was perceived as if demons had themselves instantaneously undertaken an oath to carry out the curses attached to them.

The ancients also believed that cultic and ethical sin left a residue of "impurity" or "pollution." By these terms the ancients did not mean some kind of physical dirt or a metaphoric idea but rather the attraction of demons: a dangerous metaphysical "fallout" that jeopardized the very foundations of human life.[4] In their view, human sin unleashed punishing, demonic forces:[5]

---

4. Beyerlin observes, "The close interweaving of state and cult is expressed in the high-priestly function of the king at many important divine festivals which were held throughout the land, and in his ultimate responsibility for national catastrophes (including natural disasters and epidemics). It was in accordance with this exposed position of the ruler that he was particularly concerned to protect himself against chance ritual impurity or ritual impurity conjured up by black magic, as against anything introduced from outside which would incur divine anger or misfortune." Walter Beyerlin, *Near Eastern Religious Texts Relating to the Old Testament* (Philadelphia: Westminster Press, 1978), 148–149.

5. The notion that sin attracted demons can also be illustrated from biblical literature. Genesis 4:7 is usually rendered, "Sin (*rovetz*) crouches at the door." But in Ugaritic *rabitzu* is the proper name of a demon who would lay in wait for his victim outside the door. The Hebrew *rovetz* is not a verb but a participle functioning as a noun. Genesis 4:7 would more accurately be translated as, "Sin is a demon at the door." In modern parlance we might equate the image of the attraction of demons with the radioactive "fall-out" from a nuclear disaster.

In the minds of the ancients there was a close connection between the notion of purity or cleanness and the notion of being
consecrated to God. There was a mysterious and frightening
force inherent in things that were impure and in things that were
sacred, and these two forces acted on everything with which they
came into contact, placing the objects or persons that touched
them under a kind of interdict. . . . Yet this impurity is not to be
understood as a physical or moral defilement. . . .[6]

The proliferation of demonic forces in the world could lead to
national catastrophe because they might cause God to leave the
Temple:

[The priestly sacrificial cult] presumes that sin is a miasma which
wherever committed is attracted to the sanctuary. There it adheres
and accumulates until God will no longer abide in it. Hence, it is
forever incumbent upon Israel, through the indispensible medium
of priesthood, to purge the sanctuary regularly of its impurities lest
God abandon it and the people to their doom.[7]

For these reasons it was very important to get rid of troublesome
demons or, at least in some other way, to neutralize their power. The
principal countermeasures against demons were through purgations,
banishments, and incantations.

Scholars are divided on the function of the biblical Yom Kippur.
Claiming that "the world of demons is nonexistent" for Israelite religion, Milgrom argues that the identification of ritual impurity with
demonic powers was central to the polytheistic religions of the ancient
Near East, but incompatible with Israelite monotheism. In his view
the blood of the slain animals purged the Temple of its impurities,
and the scapegoat carried away the people's sins.[8]

---

6. De Vaux, *Ancient Israel*, 460.

7. Jacob Milgrom, "Kipper," in *Encyclopaedia Judaica*, 1972 ed.

8. Jacob Milgrom, "Day of Atonement," in *Encyclopaedia Judaica*, 1972
ed. Milgrom has also shown that the word *kipper*, in the context of ritual

Far more likely, however, is the view that the central focus of the biblical Yom Kippur was the purgation and banishment of demons. The blood of the two sacrificed animals, which was sprinkled and smeared in the Holy of Holies, functioned to neutralize the powers of demons generated by sin and cultic error within the Temple complex (Leviticus 16:16, 19). Levine describes the dynamic of the situation:

> Such use of blood was also apotropaic, but the force of the blood was not directed at the deity being worshipped but at demonic powers which threatened him. The offenses, which had necessitated the expiatory sacrifices in the first instance, had unleashed these demonic powers, and had allowed them to penetrate the Israelite community where the deity resided. They threatened the purity of his sanctuary residence, and had to be driven out. They accepted the blood offered to them and withdrew. This is the purpose of the dabbing of sacrificial blood on the horns of the altar of incense, and on other cultic furnishings, which stood on the route of entry into the innermost precincts of the sanctuary. The defilement of these inner precincts might endanger the purity of the resident deity and induce him to withdraw."[9]

The banishment of the live goat (scapegoat) to Azazel functioned to expel the demons from the Temple and prevent them from returning (Leviticus 14:4–7, 16:21). This understanding has been illuminated further by the discovery that Azazel is the name of a demon assumed to live in the wilderness (Leviticus 13:21). Thus the purpose of this ritual was to banish the demons to their original source.[10]

---

impurity, meant to purge "by rubbing off." The smearing or sprinkling of the animal blood upon the horns of the altar absorbed the ritual impurity and thereby purged the Temple of contamination. See idem, "Kipper," 1039.

9. Baruch Levine, prolegomenon to Gray, *Sacrifice in the Old Testament*, xxviii.

10. Shmuel Ahituv, "Azazel," in *Encyclopaedia Judaica*, 1972 ed. The symbol of banishment is also found in the Babylonian New Year Festival (Akitu),

Another principal way to get rid of demons was the process of incantation. An incantation can be defined as

> the authorized use of rhythmically organized words of power that are chanted, spoken, or written to accomplish a desired goal by binding spiritual powers to act in a favorable way.[11]

Most incantations are defensive in nature, attempting to frustrate the hostile designs of demons against human beings. But we also find productive incantations that compel demons to help in efforts such as healing, fertility, love, sexual attraction, and successful childbirth.

Magical incantations presume that vows and oaths are as binding upon the world of demons as they are on human affairs. Just as one party can compel another to provide testimony under oath in a court of law, so, too, incantations work by forcing demons to swear vows or oaths.[12] Note the frequent use of the terms "to tie," "to bind," "to shackle," as a metaphor to render demons harmless. The image here is not, as originally thought, one of stopping demons by literally tying them up. For how would that help you get rid of them? Rather the idea is that demons will be "bound" by oath to obey human bidding. Indeed, the technical meaning for the word *exorcism* is "to expel a demon by causing it to swear an oath."

Exorcisms have the power to bind and compel demons to undertake oaths of banishment and exile:

---

where the climax of the festival involved the purification (kupparu) of the Temple through the sacrifice of a ram. Its body was thrown into the river and its head into the "open country." See "Temple Program for the New Year Festival," in James P. Pritchard, ed., *Ancient Near Eastern Texts Relating to the Old Testament* (Princeton: Princeton University Press, 1969), 333.

11. Theodore M. Ludwig, "Incantations," in *The Encyclopedia of Religion*, 1987 ed.

12. Buchanan, "Some Vow and Oath Formulas," 324–325; Greenberg, "Oaths," 1297.

In the name of the Lord of salvations. Designated is this bowl for the sealing of the house of this Geyonai bar Mamai, that there flee from him the evil Lilith, in the name of "YHWH El has scattered"; the Lilith, the male Lilis and the female Liliths, the Hag, and the Ghul. . . . Hear and obey and come forth from the house and the dwelling of this Geyonai bar Mamai and from Rasnoi his wife, the daughter of Marath. I place you under oath (*umit 'a likhin*) by the honor of your father and by the honor of your mother. . . . I make you swear (*mashb'ana likhin*) by the Strong One of Abraham, by the Rock of Isaac, by the Shaddai of Jacob . . . to turn away from this Rasnoi, daughter of Marath and from Geyonai, her husband.[13]

and

In thy name, O Lord of salvations, the great Savior of love. Designated is this spell and mystery and strong seal for the sealing of the household of this Ardoi bar Hormizduch, that from him may depart and remove the evil demon and the evil satan, who is called SP'SK, the Mighty Destroyer, who kills a man from the side of his wife and a woman from the side of her husband, and sons and daughters from their father and from their mother. . . . I make you swear (*mashb'ana 'alakh*) that you do not kill off this Ardoi bar Hormizduch from Ahath his wife, and that thou do not kill off Ahath bat Parkoi from Ardoi her husband, and that thou do not kill off their sons and their daughters, whether those they have or those they shall have, from this day and forever, neither by night nor by day.[14]

---

13. Montgomery, *Aramaic Incantation Texts*, 154–160; this incantation is cited by Jacob Neusner in *A History of the Jews in Babylonia*, vol. 6, 220; see also Baruch Levine, "Appendix: The Language of the Magic Bowls," in Neusner's *A History of the Jews in Babylonia*, vol. 5 (Leiden: E. J. Brill, 1970), 347–351.

14. Montgomery, *Aramaic Incantation Texts*, 127–132.

Exorcisms are frequently attested in Christian sources as well. Jesus is frequently portrayed in the New Testament as casting out demons by the spirit of God or by prayer from the bodies of the "possessed":

Then a blind and dumb demoniac was brought to him, and he healed him, so that the dumb man spoke and saw. And all the people were amazed, and said, "Can this be the Son of David?" But when the Pharisees heard it they said, "It is only by Beelzebul, the prince of demons, that this man cast out demons." . . . He said to them, ". . . But if it is by the Spirit of God that I cast out demons, then the kingdom of God has come upon you" (Matthew 12:22–28).

and

And one of the crowd answered him, "Teacher, I brought my son to you, for he has a dumb spirit; and whenever, it dashes him down; and he foams and grinds his teeth and becomes rigid; and I asked your disciples to cast it out, and they were not able." . . . (Jesus) rebuked the unclean spirit, saying to it, "You deaf and dumb spirit, I command you, come out of him, and never enter him again." . . . His disciples asked him privately, "Why could we not cast it out?" And he said to them, "This kind cannot be driven out by anything but prayer" (Mark 9:17–29).[15]

Jesus' disciples, the clergy, and lay Christians, however, conducted exorcisms principally by "the solemn and authoritative adjuration addressed to the demon in the name of God, and more especially in the name of Christ crucified," along with the laying of hands on the subject and making the sign of the cross.[16]

---

15. Cf. Matthew 8:16, 15:22–28; Mark 1:23–26, 3:22; Luke 11:20.

16. P. J. Toner, "Exorcism," in *The Catholic Encyclopedia*, 1909 ed.

We can now state our understanding of magical incantations even more precisely than we did in Chapter Two. Magic did not merely influence the will of demons and other supernatural beings. The image of magic held by the ancients was far more concrete. The conception underlying magic in antiquity was crystallized by the formula found in a Greek magical papyrus cited by Lieberman: "I bind, I bind."[17] He interpreted this twofold repetition to imply "I bind [through magic]" and "I bind [through oath]." In Lieberman's own words,

> [magical incantations] arrogated to themselves the power to compel the victim of the magical act to do the will of the adjuror.[18]

Believing in the power of vows and oaths to bind humans and demons alike, the practitioners of magic applied many legal formulae to bind commitments in the human world to the demonic realm. Among the most popular of these procedures was the nullification of vows.

---

17. Lieberman, "Adjurations in Israel," 28.
18. Ibid.

6

Kol Nidrei
and Incantation Texts

Neusner, Trachtenberg, and Lieberman have demonstrated the significant place of demonology in the life of Babylonian Jewry during the talmudic period.[1] Jewish demonology flourished in the cultural climate of Babylonia where Persian dualism and the belief in demons was widespread:[2]

> Gentiles and Jews alike wanted to be saved from demons and from illnesses, to exorcise ghosts, and, especially, to preserve the happiness of their marital life. Both groups believed demons had a particularly ill affect on these matters, and both looked forward

---

1. Neusner, *A History of the Jews in Babylonia*, vol. 5, 336–341; Trachtenberg, *Jewish Magic and Superstition*; Lieberman, "Pleasures and Fears," in *Greek*, 97–114.

2. J. Bruce Long, "Demons," in *Encyclopedia of Religion*, 1987 ed. In Jewish demonology demons were known as both a generic class and as individuals. Some generic names for demons were *lilit* (female demons), *shedim* (devils), *mazzikim* (injurers), *ruchot* (spirits), and *malachei chabbalah* (angels of destruction). Other demons were given proper names. Asmodeus or Samael was the king of the demons, and Igrat bat Machalat was the queen. See *The Encyclopedia of the Jewish Religion*, 1966 ed., s.v. "Demonology."

to a salvation which consisted of good health, sexual satisfaction, and normal daily life unmarred by inexplicable accidents or bad luck. No one seems to have enjoyed an abundance of such bless-ings.[3]

Apparently Jews had something of a reputation in the talmudic period for their magical skills. The second-century *Tanna* Simeon bar Yohai bragged about Jewish expertise in the magical arts:

> The Master says: We do not pass by food [which is lying in the street and which may have been used for protection against spirits]. R. Yochanan in the name of R. Simeon bar Yohai says: This decision applies only to the earlier generations, when the daughters of Israel were not practiced in all arts of magic; but nowadays, when the daughters of Israel are indeed practiced in all magical arts, this does not apply . . . (B. T. *Eruvin* 64b).

In addition to prayer, amulets, and incantations, the Jews be-lieved themselves to possess another potent weapon against demons—the study of Torah and the practice of commandments:

> R. Joseph said that a commandment protects and rescues [from demons] when one is doing it, but afterwards, while it protects, it does not rescue. Rava said that while one is engaged in study of Torah, the act of study protects and rescues, but otherwise, study of Torah protects but does not rescue. As to a command-ment, under all circumstances it protects but does not rescue (B. T. *Sotah* 21a).

The belief in demons was not limited to folk religion. The rab-bis accepted the reality of demons as well. Indeed, as "holy men," rabbis were expected to be adept at controlling demons and manipu-lating them to perform human bidding. Neusner has described the

---

3. Neusner, A *History of the Jews in Babylonia*, vol. 6, 242–243.

talmudic rabbi as a "lawyer-magician" who was able by virtue of his knowledge of the Torah and divine names to work miracles, interpret dreams, exorcise demons, compose healing incantations, and manufacture amulets:[4]

> 'Igrat daughter of Machalat, queen of demons, once met Abbaye. She said to him, "Had they not proclaimed concerning you in heaven, 'Take heed of Nahmani and his Torah,' I would have endangered you." He replied, "If I am important in heaven, I order you never to pass through inhabited areas" (B. T. *Pesachim* 112b).

While the majority of rabbis probably accepted the reality of demons and the efficacy of magic, not all of them approved of the latter's use. Some must have found magic to be idolatrous, inconsistent with Jewish belief in divine sovereignty, reward and punishment, and human free will.[5] Yet Lieberman's portrayal of the rabbis as engaged in a battle with the masses over magic is overdone for "popular beliefs are always represented in the establishment."[6]

Jewish demonology is known principally through the study of the Babylonian Talmud. Since 1853, however, more than 100 magical incantations inscribed on earthenware bowls were discovered in Babylonia, principally at Nippur, but also at other sites in the Middle East. These incantation texts dating from the fourth to the seventh century C.E. were roughly contemporaneous with the formation of the Talmud. They are written primarily in Aramaic, Mandaic, and Syriac:

> These texts are inscribed spirally in black ink on the interior (and sometimes exterior) surface of clay dishes approximately a porridge bowl in size and shape. The scribe sometimes added a crude

---

4. Jacob Neusner, "The Phenomenon of the Rabbi in Late Antiquity," *Numen* 16 (April 1969): 1–20.

5. Lieberman, *Greek*, 91–113.

6. Personal communication from Dr. Baruch Levine.

drawing (usually in the center) often depicting the demon(s) to be foiled by the incantation.[7]

Gold suggests that the continuous spiral of the incantation text is symbolic of how the magical formula binds the demon as if in a web.[8]

Most of these bowls were found buried in homes just beneath the surface of the floor. Others were found in cemeteries. They were uniformly found in an inverted position. Gordon suggests that the power of the incantation inhered not only in the words them-selves but in the symbolism of the inverted bowl. Just as the bowl was overturned, so too, the plans of the evil forces would also be over-turned.[9] But Gold speculates that the bowls were inverted so that the incantation texts would face in the direction of where the demons resided. They would then read the texts on their way up to the human world.[10]

These Babylonian magic bowls have shed new light on the reli-gious praxis of Babylonian Jewry, particularly with regard to *kol nidrei*.[11] Gordon noticed that the magic bowl incantations texts closely paralleled the structure and language of *kol nidrei*. They were writ-ten in the same style as a legal nullification of vows, the difference being that they nullified not vows but curses and spells. Gordon also noticed that many Aramaic terms used in *kol nidrei* had parallels in

---

7. Cyrus H. Gordon, "Leviathan: Symbol of Evil," in *Biblical Motifs: Origins and Transformations*, ed. Alexander Altmann (Cambridge: Harvard Univerity Press, 1966), 5.

8. Personal communication from Rabbi Manuel Gold.

9. Gordon, "Leviathan," 6–7.

10. Personal communication from Rabbi Manuel Gold.

11. Herr writes, "The remarkable similarity between the *Kol Nidre* formula and the formulae of the magical incantations cannot be ignored." See Moshe David Herr, "Matters of Palestinian *Halakhah* During the Sixth and Seventh Centuries c.e.," [Hebrew] *Tarbitz* 48 (October 1979–March 1980), vi.

the incantations: *nidrei, isarei, shivei, cheremei, shevitin, shevikin, sharirin, kayamin, bitalin.*[12]

Remarkably, some of these incantations utilized the very words "*kol nidrei*":

> Health and protection and healing from the heavens let there be unto Shiroy, son of Burzin, or any name that the son of Burzin may have. Blessed be the Lord of creatures! by this countercharm do I disenchant and in the name of this True One do annul all vows (*kol nidrei*) and curses and knocks and spells. . . . He who cancels (*miftar*) the vows (*nidrei*) of mankind and the decree of heaven, He will annul (*yabtil*) these vows (*nidrei*).[13]

and

> Upset, upset is the earth. Upset is the earth. . . . Upset are all the vows (*kol nidrei*) and curses, spells and magic, curses and magic and evil blows that may lodge in this man.[14]

Montgomery published magic bowl inscriptions that utilized *kol nidrei* terms such as *shevikin*, and *sharirin* also. The term *shevikin* is attested in the magic bowl inscriptions to refer to a bill of divorce given to female demons in order to banish them from a human home:

> I [Joshua bar Perachia] write for them divorces, for all the Liliths who appear to them in this house of Babanos bar Kayomta and

12. Gordon, "Leviathan," 6–7 n. 23. See the glossary compiled by William H. Rossell, *A Handbook of Aramaic Magical Texts*, Shelton Semitic Series Number II (Ringwood Borough, NJ: Shelton College, 1953), 122–153.

13. Cyrus Gordon, "Aramaic Incantation Bowls," *Orientalia* 10 (1941): 341–342.

14. Cyrus Gordon, "Leviathan," 6–7.

of Saradust bat Sirin his wife . . . a writ of separation and divorce (*degita dape vidishivukin*).[15]

and

This day above any day, years of generations of the world, I Komes bat Mahlaphta have divorced (*shevikit*), separated, dismissed thee, thou Lilith, Lilith of the Desert.[16]

The term *kayam v'sharir* was employed in the magic bowls to certify that an incantation against demons was valid and in force, having been sealed by God:

In the name of YHWH-in Yah, El-el the great, the awful, whose word is panacea, this mystery is confirmed, made fast and sure (*kayam vesharir*), forever and ever.[17]

All these texts show how authors of these incantations believed that the legal terminology for contracts, bills of divorce, and the nullification of vows in the human world were equally efficacious in the realm of demons.

On the basis of these linguistic and conceptual parallels between magic bowl incantation texts and *kol nidrei*, Gordon concluded that *kol nidrei* must also have served in a magical context. That is, the language of *kol nidrei* operated on two levels, the mundane and the magical. The terminology for the various types of human vows, when transposed into a magical key, had a radically different meaning. For

---

15. Montgomery, *Ancient Incantation Texts*, 161. Joshua ben Perachiah was frequently mentioned in the Babylonian magic bowls. He was known to exorcise female demons by issuing them bills of divorce. See the discussion of him in Neusner, "The Phenomenon of the Rabbi in Late Antiquity," 13–17, and in Neusner, *A History of the Jews in Babylonia*, vol. 6, 235–243.

16. Montgomery, *Aramaic Incantation Texts*, 190.

17. Ibid., 178.

example, the word *neder* means "vow." But in a magical context, it meant "curse." *Isar* means "prohibitive vow," but also "spell." *Shevuah* means "oath," but also "curse." *Cherem* means "dedicatory vow," but also "ban." In Gordon's view, *kol nidrei* functioned as an incantation that nullified curses and spells:

> The original function of the prayer was the annulment of curses or oaths (originally *not* in the sense of promises or contractual obligations) that touch off evil forces in the community . . . its purpose is to give the community a fresh start by annulling the evil forces set in motion by destructive (even if unpremeditated) words.[18]

Thus Gordon held that *kol nidrei* did not annul human vows at all.[19] *Kol nidrei* functioned as an incantation that nullified the whole range of curses and spells people bring upon themselves and each other.

The notion that *kol nidrei* refers to curses and not to human vows is given additional credence by Trachtenberg's discovery that the phrase "with the consent of X" is a common preamble for the nullification of curses and exorcisms against demons:

> With the consent of the heavenly and earthly courts, of our sacred Torah, of the great and small Sanhedrins, and of this holy congregation, we release N son of N from all the curses, maledictions, oaths, vows . . . uttered in his home, or directed against him or any member of his household, be they his own curses or the curses of others against his person, or curses that he uttered against others, unwarrantedly or deservedly, in a moment of wrath or with malice prepense, intentionally or unintentionally,

---

18. Gordon, "Leviathan," 5–6 n. 23.

19. Rabbi Manuel Gold suggests that *kol nidrei*'s failure to fulfill the talmudic requirements for the nullification of human vows is a sure tip-off that its author had never intended it for that purpose.

whatever their occasion or character. With the consent of God
and of His celestial and terrestrial menage, let them all be null
and void, like unto a clay vessel that has been shattered.[20]

Gold suggests that *kol nidrei* functioned in tandem with a *hatarat nedarim* on Yom Kippur eve.[21] He proposes that the nullification of vows took care of the human vows but had no power over
curses, whether of the self-imposed or externally directed variety.
Kol nidrei served as an incantation that successfully nullified all these
curses.

Gold's hypothesis of a tandem ritual on Yom Kippur eve receives
additional support from the unpublished incantation cited by Shlomo
Deshen discussed in Chapter Five.[22] This undated manuscript described the Yom Kippur eve practice in Cheven, a city on the Arabian
peninsula near Yemen. We are told that the ritual began with *kol
nidrei*, followed by "the consent of Elijah," which nullifies "every vow
and oath that causes punishment upon a human being." The service
concluded with an incantation releasing the demons from all the oaths
that had been imposed upon them. Consistent with Gold's hypothesis, the Yom Kippur eve ritual in Cheven did indeed appear to involve a nullification of human vows and a nullification of curses,
charms, and spells.

Levine rejects the interpretation of Gordon and Gold.[23] He
maintains that *kol nidrei* did not function as a magical incantation
and had nothing to do with curses. He argues that *kol nidrei* served
liturgically to nullify the unfulfilled vows and oaths of remorseful

---

20. Trachtenberg, *Jewish Magic and Superstition*, 60, 158.

21. Personal communication from Rabbi Manuel Gold.

22. Deshen ("The Enigma of *Kol Nidre*," 145–146) presumes that *kol
nidrei* was indeed an incantation whose purpose was to expel demons prior
to the especially vulnerable time of Yom Kippur, the Day of Judgment.
Deshen believes this hypothesis provides an explanation for why *kol nidrei*
figures so prominently at the beginning of the Yom Kippur eve service.

23. Personal communication from Dr. Baruch Levine.

people who sought to reconcile themselves with God and to escape divine punishment implemented by demons.

While *kol nidrei* may have been perceived by some elements within the folk as a magical incantation against curses, Levine contends that neither the rabbis nor the majority of the folk ever lost sight of *kol nidrei*'s moorings as a legal fiction for the nullification of human vows. In contrast to Gold and Gordon, Levine believes that *kol nidrei* was never transformed into a "magical key," despite its many linguistic parallels with the Babylonian incantation texts.

7
Kol Nidrei's Place of Origin

Early twentieth century scholarship tended toward the conclusion that *kol nidrei* was originally a Palestinian custom that subsequently won widespread popularity in Babylonia.[1] This hypothesis was primarily based upon the responsum of Natronai bar Hillai (of Sura, 853–858) which claimed that *kol nidrei* was not practiced in Babylonia:

> We do not practice in the two academies nor anywhere else to annul vows, neither on Rosh haShanah nor on Yom Kippur. However, we have heard that in other countries they say "all vows (*kol nidrei*) and prohibitions," but we have neither seen nor

---

1. Hoffman cites Poznanski, Elbogen, and Mann. Since Poznanski and Elbogen wrote in German, I am relying upon Hoffman's research. Lawrence A. Hoffman, *The Canonization of the Synagogue Service* (Notre Dame: University of Notre Dame Press, 1979), 215 n. 39. Mann (*Texts and Studies*, 53) argued for the Palestinian origin of *kol nidrei* on the grounds that the practice was attacked by the Jerusalem Karaites in the ninth century. I fail to grasp what this datum proves since the Babylonian *Geonim* also attacked *kol nidrei* in the same century. See also Herr, "Matters of Palestinian *Halakhah*," 70.

heard of it [i.e., no such tradition has been passed down to us] from our rabbis.[2]

But Natronai's assertion that *kol nidrei* was not practiced in Babylonia has been contradicted by at least two other sources, which explicitly report that *kol nidrei* or some form of *hatarat nedarim* was practiced by the public in Babylonia. Hai bar Nachshon (of Sura, 885–896) stated:

> It is the practice of the people in our region to say on Yom Kippur "all vows" (*kol nidrei*) and to say legal fictions (*divrei ha'aramah*) for the coming year.[3]

We find also in *Pirkei Ben Baboi*, an eighth-century tractate composed by a disciple of Yehudai Gaon:

> Before Yehudai forbade [the nullification of vows on Rosh haShanah and Yom Kippur], they were already complying in the provinces but not in the little towns. But ever since Yehudai's prohibition, vows and oaths are not nullified even in the little towns, and whoever vows fulfills his vow and whoever swears fulfills his oath.[4]

Even Hai Gaon himself conceded in another responsum that some *Geonim* approved *kol nidrei* and other types of *hatarat nedarim*:

> We have seen people in countries practising according to this *mishnah* [M. *Nedarim* 3:1], upon whose authority a few *Geonim* have relied to perform legal fictions (*ha'aramot*) and *charatot* on Yom Kippur eve.[5]

---

2. Benjamin Lewin, ed., *Otsar haGeonim*, vol. 11 (Jerusalem, 1928–1942), *Nedarim*, #63; cf. #57.

3. Wolf Leiter, ed., *Sha'arei Teshuvah* (1802; reprint ed., New York: Philipp Feldheim, 1946), *Nedarim*, #143.

4. Shraga Abramson, "Blessing for the Cancellation of Vows and Oaths," 185.

5. Leiter, *Sha'arei Teshuvah*, *Nedarim*, #143.

Thus far, our sources contradict each other about whether *kol nidrei* was practiced in Babylonia. It may well be, however, that Natronai's statement has been misinterpreted. Upon closer examination, it is possible to understand Natronai's remarks as primarily emphasizing that *kol nidrei* was not practiced at the *academies* and *should* not be practiced anywhere else because the sages had no prior tradition authorizing it. If this reading is correct, then all the sources cited above agree that *kol nidrei* was practiced in Babylonia. It also means that Natronai's responsum cannot be employed in defense of the Palestinian origin for *kol nidrei*. At the same time, however, the fact that *kol nidrei* was practiced in Babylonia does not necessarily imply that it originated there.

Another argument for the Palestinian origin of *kol nidrei* is Deshen's observation that the language of Hai Gaon's *kol nidrei* points to the influence of Palestinian Aramaic.[6] White points out that several items in Hai's *kol nidrei* reflect Palestinian usage. Among these are the utilization of *sherei* (release) and *shevak* (forgive) as a pair; *beshalu* (unintentionally); *'onsa* (unavoidable circumstance); *bedilhon* (on account of them).[7]

While Hai Gaon's *kol nidrei* may in fact incorporate elements of Palestinian Aramaic, this does not conclusively demonstrate that it originated in Palestine. Given the decline of Aramaic with the rise of Islam, White suggests that Hai Gaon may simply have written the *kol nidrei* formula in what he considered at the time to be good Aramaic. In addition, Deshen notes that *shevitin* and *shevikin* frequently occur in Babylonian sources. Most probably Hai Gaon's *kol nidrei* is a conflation of Palestinian and Babylonian Aramaic. Nothing definitive can be learned from it about *kol nidrei*'s place of origin.

As discussed in Chapter Three, by the eighth century some people were deriving the practice of *kol nidrei* from B. *Talmud Nedarim* 23b. The *mishnah* discussed by that *gemara* is *Mishnah Nedarim* 3:1:

---

6. Deshen, "The Enigma of *Kol Nidre*," 147 n. 17.
7. Personal communication from Dr. Richard White.

He who desires that none of his vows made during the year shall be valid, let him stand at Rosh haShanah and declare, "Every vow that I may make in the future shall be null."

While acknowledging that *kol nidrei* and the practice described above are two different customs, some argue that the Palestinian origin of this mishnaic practice implies the Palestinian origin of *kol nidrei* as well. But even if we grant the Palestinian provenance of the *Mishnah*, it still does not follow that *kol nidrei* originated in Palestine. Babylonian Jews knew the *Mishnah* too and could have invented *kol nidrei* just as much as the Palestinians.

So far then we have little evidence—certainly no conclusive evidence—to support the conclusion that *kol nidrei* originated in Palestine.[8] Except for Abramson, most recent scholarship since the 1960s tends to the conclusion that *kol nidrei* originated in Babylonia.[9]

Herr argues that the line of transmission for *kol nidrei* and for the custom of abrogating vows on Rosh haShanah in general must have originated in the cultural climate of Babylonia, where such practices were rife.[10] He claims that *kol nidrei* was initially developed in Babylonia by the folk as a communal nullification of vows. Herr maintains that *kol nidrei* reached Palestine at the end of the sixth or seventh century. Along with Gordon and Deshen, Herr contends that the similarities between *kol nidrei* and the Babylonian incantation texts conclusively prove that *kol nidrei* is originally of Babylonian provenance.

---

8. Herr ("Matters of Palestinian *Halakhah*," 70) expresses the same evaluation.

9. See Chapter Four, p. 34 n. 16.

10. Herr, "Matters of Palestinian *Halakhah*," 70–75.

III

KOL NIDREI
IN HISTORICAL
INTERACTION

8

The Babylonian *Geonim* and *Kol Nidrei*

The Babylonian *Geonim* were certainly aware of *kol nidrei's* popularity in folk religion as an incantation against demons. Except for the brief remark of Rav Amram, however, the *Geonim* uniformly declined to refer to *kol nidrei* as a magical incantation. They described it as a nullification of human vows and expressed their approval or disapproval of it on legal grounds.

The Babylonian *Geonim* did not adopt a monolithic stance with regard to *kol nidrei*. Natronai, Amram, and Hai bar Nachshon condemned the recitation of *kol nidrei*. Saadia permitted it under specific circumstances. Hai bar Sherira approved only his own version of *kol nidrei*. Paltoi may have permitted it outright. In addition to this data, there are sources in both *Sha'arei Teshuvah* and *Shibbolei haLeket* that claim that other unnamed *Geonim* favored *kol nidrei*.

Aptowitzer was the first to contend that the *Geonim* of Pumbedita were lenient with respect to the annulment of vows, while the *Geonim* of Sura were stringent.[1] While this theory may not be totally

---

1. Aptowitzer was supported in this opinion by Ginzberg, Kieval, and Baron. But Mann believed that the purported difference was erroneous. See Louis Ginzberg, *Ginzei Schechter*, vol. 2 (1929; reprint ed., New York: Jew-

correct, there was a strong movement against the nullification of vows in Sura by the time of Yehudai (757–761).

Yehudai declared that neither academy would nullify vows or even study the talmudic tractate on vows because they did not feel competent to deal with the subject:

> We do not revoke vows or annul oaths because we have not expounded upon the talmudic tractate for vows in more than 100 years. . . . We do not comprehend the profundity of these matters and we do not have the authority to annul vows, much less to annul oaths. It is not practiced at the two academies or anywhere else in all of Babylonia to revoke vows and to annul oaths. . . . There is no sage in this generation who knows how to revoke vows and to annul prohibitive vows. Likewise, you too should be strict with regard to vows, and with oaths all the more so, and don't deviate from the custom of the academies.[2]

The earliest Gaon specifically to express opposition to *kol nidrei* was Natronai bar Hillai (of Sura, 853–858):

> We do not practice in the two academies or anywhere else to annul vows, neither on Rosh haShanah nor on Yom Kippur. However, we have heard that in other countries they say "all vows (*kol nidrei*) and prohibitions," but we have neither seen nor heard of it from our rabbis.[3]

---

ish Theological Seminary, 1969), 120; Kieval, "The Curious Case of *Kol Nidre*," 55; and Salo Baron, *Philosophy and Science*, vol. 8, *A Social and Religious History of the Jews* (New York: Columbia University Press, 1958), 78; Mann, *Texts and Studies*, 52 n. 99.

2. Lewin, *Otsar haGeonim*, vol. 11, *Nedarim*, #56; *Orchot Chayyim, Hilkhot Yom haKippurim* #29.

3. Lewin, *Otsar haGeonim*, vol. 11, *Nedarim*, #63; cf. *Sha'arei Simchah*, vol. 1, 60; *Rosh to Yoma 88b* end; *Tur, Orach Chayyim* 619; *Orchot Chayyim, Hilkhot Yom haKippurim* #29.

Natronai's opposition to *kol nidrei* was not based solely on the absence of a positive precedent for it. He believed in fact that an actual *negative* precedent existed in Jewish tradition. From Rava's opposition to educating the public about the anticipatory invalidation of future vows, Natronai inferred that he would have been even more opposed to the nullification of past vows, and thus also to *kol nidrei*:

> If Rava did not believe that the law allowing for the anticipatory invalidation of future vows should be taught to the public, all the more so one should not annul, or teach about how to annul, vows and oaths that were already undertaken . . . thus we do not accept nor do we practice this *hatarah*.[4]

Natronai's opposition to *kol nidrei* was strengthened by Amram (858–871), his successor at Sura. After citing the text of *kol nidrei* in his prayer book, Amram remarked without further elaboration:

> But the holy academy sent word that this is a foolish custom and it is forbidden to practice it.[5]

Beyond Amram's cursory remark, there is no other known rabbinic statement directly critical of *kol nidrei* as a magical incantation. However, the Rambam used the exact same term ("foolish") to describe those who converted the *mezuzah* into a magical amulet:

> They, however, who write names of angels, holy names, a biblical text, or inscriptions usual on seals within the *mezuzah*, are among those who have no portion in the world to come. For these fools not only fail to fulfill the commandment but they

---

4. I have not yet found this statement in the Geonic sources. It was attributed to Natronai by the Rosh (Rosh to *Yoma* 88b end); the *Tur, Orach Chayyim* 619; and *Sefer haManhig, Hilkhot Tzom Kippur* #56.

5. Goldschmidt, *Seder Rav Amram Gaon*, 163.

treat an important precept that expresses the Unity of God, the love of Him, and His worship, as if it were an amulet to promote their own personal interests; for, according to their foolish minds, the *mezuzah* is something that will secure for them advantage in the vanities of the world.[6]

The position of Saadia Gaon (of Sura, 928–942) toward *kol nidrei* was somewhat more complex. He did not include *kol nidrei* in his prayer book.[7] Saadia did, however, allow the formula to be used on an *ad hoc* basis to annul vows made in error by entire congregations, but not by individuals:

> By rabbinic ordinance a community may say *kol nidrei* that has made a mistake and imposed upon themselves a prohibition in the synagogue, such as vows that cannot be fulfilled due to unavoidable circumstances and communal errors, as it is written, "If it is the whole community of Israel that has erred . . ." (Leviticus 4:13). But someone that had sworn for the entire year to release his oaths and to annul them, no.[8]

The next Gaon to condemn *kol nidrei* was Hai bar Nachshon (of Sura, 885–896):

> The law is according to Rava [who ruled that the anticipatory invalidation of future vows should not be taught to the public].

---

6. Rambam, *Mishneh Torah, Hilkhot Mezuzah* 5:4.

7. Mann (*Texts and Studies*, 52 n. 99) erroneously asserted that *kol nidrei* was included in Saadia's prayer book. Based upon a Spanish and Yemenite tradition that Saadia approved *kol nidrei*, Baron claims that Saadia had decided in favor of *kol nidrei* in a "special responsum since lost." See Salo Baron, *Hebrew Language and Letters*, vol. 7, *A Social and Religious History of the Jews* (New York: Columbia University Press, 1958), 252 n. 20.

8. Lewin, *Otsar haGeonim*, vol. 11, *Nedarim*, #62; cf. *Sha'arei Simchah*, Volume One, p. 60; *Tur, Orach Chayyim* 619; *Orchot Chayyim, Hilchot Yom haKippurim* #29.

Therefore we do not act according to this *mishnah* [M. *Nedarim* 3:1]. We do not revoke vows, neither on Rosh haShanah nor on Yom Kippur. We have not heard from our rabbis about this prac-tice at all. Likewise, you too should be strict and not deviate from the custom of the academies.[9]

However, Hai acknowledged elsewhere that some *Geonim* had supported the practice of *hatarat nedarim*:

We have seen people in countries practicing according to this *mishnah* [M. *Nedarim* 3:1], upon whose authority a few *Geonim* have relied to perform *ha'aramot* (legal fictions) and *charatot* on Yom Kippur eve. . . . You too should be strict and conform to the custom of the *chasidim harishonim* (early pietists) and not devi-ate from the custom of the two academies. . . . It is a grave mat-ter [to abrogate] a vow or an oath, God forbid.[10]

The first Gaon specifically to approve of *kol nidrei* on a regular basis was Paltoi (of Pumbedita, 842–857):

It is our custom and that of *Beit Rabbenu* in Babylonia that the prayer leader says *shehecheyanu* and then *kol nidrei* and then *borchu*.[11]

---

9. Lewin, *Otsar haGeonim*, vol. 11, *Nedarim*, #66; cf. *Sha'arei Simchah*, vol. 1, 60; Rosh to *Yoma* 88b end; *Tur*, *Orach Chayyim* 619; *Orchot Chayyim*, *Hilkhot Yom haKippurim* #29.

10. Leiter, *Sha'arei haTeshuvah*, *Nedarim*, #143.

11. Lewin, *Otsar haGeonim*, vol. 11, *Nedarim*, #64. Poznanski and Mann (*Texts and Studies*, 52 n. 99) discounted this responsum on the grounds that the reference to *kol nidrei* was a later interpolation. But Baron accepted it as authentic. See Salo Baron, *Laws, Homilies, and the Bible*, vol. 6, *A Social and Religious History of the Jews* (New York: Columbia University Press, 1958), 389 n. 143.

The only other Gaon known to have approved *kol nidrei* was Hai
bar Sherira (of Pumbedita, 998–1038). But Hai's approved text differed from that known to previous *Geonim*. If we can rely upon *Shibbolei haLeket*, this version of *kol nidrei* was acceptable to some other
Geonim as well:

> In the responsa of the *Geonim* I found that most of the *Geonim*
> refused to say *kol nidrei*, since it has no value besides evil, except
> for the formula of Hai Gaon. . . .[12]

Kieval speculates that the *Geonim* significantly changed their
attitude toward *kol nidrei* around the year 1000. He maintains that
by the time of Hai bar Sherira:

> Some form of *Kol Nidrei* declaration appears to have gained
> general acceptance throughout Babylonia and the far-flung
> Jewries which accepted geonic authority.[13]

But even if Kieval is correct, it was not Hai Gaon's prayer of
absolution but the Hebrew version of *kol nidrei* as a nullification of
vows that was incorporated into later prayer books. The folk must
also have recognized the difference between the two versions and
pushed for the retention of *kol nidrei* as a magical incantation.

Except for Amram's remark, the Geonic responsa uniformly
attributed their opposition to *kol nidrei* on legal grounds: (1) *kol nidrei*
was a nullification of vows they had already prohibited; (2) the practice had no precedent in rabbinic tradition; (3) *kol nidrei* violated
Rava's talmudic dictum against educating the public about procedures
to nullify vows. Beyond these explanations the Geonic sources do
not go.

Nevertheless many scholars have attempted to dig beneath the

---

12. *Shibbolei haLeket*, #317; cf. Lewin, *Otsar haGeonim*, vol. 11, *Nedarim*,
#68.

13. Kieval, "The Curious Case of *Kol Nidre*," 55.

ostensible reasons offered by the *Geonim* for their rejection of *kol nidrei* in search of other religiopolitical pressures. Baron believes that the attitude of the *Geonim* toward *kol nidrei* was influenced by the Karaites, who were opposed in principle to the nullification of vows. As Baron sees it, the *Geonim* neither totally approved nor disapproved of *kol nidrei* since either viewpoint would have given the Karaites political ammunition.[14]

Kieval contends that the *Geonim* were opposed to *kol nidrei* only insofar as it was a nullification of vows, but were prepared to accept it as a prayer for absolution. But Mann and Baron assert that the Pumbeditan *Geonim* gave in to public pressure and accepted *kol nidrei* even though it was a nullification of vows.[15] From a totally different perspective, Gordon and Deshen argue that the opposition of some *Geonim* to *kol nidrei* had little to do with its shortcomings as a nullification of vows under Jewish law. They claim that it had everything to do with Geonic opposition to *kol nidrei* as a magical incantation against demons. This theory helps also to explain why some *Geonim* accepted Hai's *kol nidrei* version and why the folk rejected it. The *Geonim* accepted his *kol nidrei* precisely because it was not a magical incantation, but a prayer for divine absolution. Conversely, the folk

---

14. Baron contends that both Natronai and Paltoi "may have been equally impressed by the growing Karaite attacks on that prayer."

On the other hand, Baron also believes that "Natronai was doubly handicapped in discouraging the *kol nidrei* prayer because he did not wish to appear as yielding to the constant Karaite assaults on that liturgical custom." Salo Baron, *Religious Controls and Dissensions*, vol. 5, *A Social and Religious History of the Jews* (New York: Columbia University Press, 1957), 249.

15. Mann (*Texts and Studies*, 52 n. 99) claimed that Hai bar Sherira "seems to have yielded to popular pressure that wanted to assure itself of a clear record on the Day of Atonement, to introduce a modified form of Kol Nidre." Baron asserts that "the *geonim* of Sura condemned the recitation of the *kol nidre* prayer . . . long after those of Pumbedita had submitted to popular clamor for it." See Salo Baron, *Philosophy and Science*, vol. 8, *A Social and Religious History of the Jews* (New York: Columbia University Press, 1958), 78.

rejected Hai's version and pushed for the retention of the *kol nidrei* known to Amram specifically because it was a magical incantation.

But even as this hypothesis seeks to answer some questions, it raises others. For example, since we know that the rabbis were not uniformly opposed to magic or the use of incantations, what was it about *kol nidrei* in particular that bothered them? And if they were opposed to *kol nidrei* as an incantation, why didn't they attack it directly?

Neither Gordon nor Deshen addressed these particular questions. But various conjectures can be proposed. To begin, the rabbis and the *Geonim* were not the same. The *Amoraim* of Sassanian Babylonia may have been more accepting of magical practices than *Geonim* living in the stringently monotheistic cultural climate of upper-class Islam.

On the other hand, the Geonic opposition to *kol nidrei* may not have been due to its magical qualities per se. Even if we presumed the existence of a Geonic spectrum of opinion on magic, many sages might have opposed the introduction of a magical incantation into communal synagogue worship, and on a day no less sacred than Yom Kippur! *Kol nidrei* would have presented a special liturgical challenge, even for those *Geonim* who favored incantations as a private praxis.

Why, then, did the *Geonim* choose not to directly attack *kol nidrei* as an inappropriate introduction of a magical incantation into the liturgy? It can be speculated that the *Geonim* may have recognized *kol nidrei* was a battle they could not win against folk religion if met head on. After all, even Rav Amram included *kol nidrei* in his prayer book. By opposing *kol nidrei* on legal grounds, the *Geonim* succeeded both in avoiding a direct clash with the public over magic and in finding an argument that would carry some weight with the public. Such a strategy is not uncommon among political institutions and establishments.

Whatever may have been the true cause of Geonic opposition to *kol nidrei*, it failed to stop the incorporation of *kol nidrei* into later prayer books and its widespread acceptance in the Medieval period throughout the Jewish world.

9

Kol Nidrei in
the Medieval Period

Despite the opposition of some Babylonian *Geonim*, the practice of *kol nidrei* was accepted during the Middle Ages by most of the Jewish communities of the world in Europe, Spain, Italy, and the Middle East.[1] This transition is reflected in the radically different treatments accorded *kol nidrei* by two eleventh-century sources. These sources are *Sha'arei Simchah*, the work of Isaac ben Judah ibn Ghiyyat (1038–1089), a halakhic authority in Lucena (Spain), and *Siddur Rabbenu Shlomo*, composed by Solomon ben Samson, a halakhic authority in Worms (Germany) and a contemporary of Rashi's German teachers, Jacob Yakar and Isaac ben Eliezer.

Ibn Ghiyyat's discussion of *kol nidrei* is quite brief.[2] He nowhere expresses his own opinion on the subject. Instead, he selectively quotes the negative Geonic opinions about *kol nidrei* of Hai bar Nachshon, Natronai, and Saadia. Taken as a whole, these sources (all of which were discussed in Chapter Eight) stress that *kol nidrei* was

---

1. Deshen ("The Enigma of *Kol Nidre*," 147) claims that Iranian Jews did not practice *kol nidrei* until the seventeenth/eighteenth centuries.

2. *Sha'arei Simchah*, ed. Simchah Bamberger, vol. 1 (Furth, 1861), *Hilkhot Yom haKippurim*, #60.

incompatible with Rava's dictum against educating the public about the nullification of vows and therefore should not be practiced at all, except for certain *ad hoc* circumstances.

In contrast, Rabbenu Shlomo holds a remarkably positive attitude toward *kol nidrei*.[3] The most surprising element of Rabbenu Shlomo's treatment of *kol nidrei* is that he didn't mention the opposition of the Babylonian *Geonim* at all. Quite the contrary, Solomon ben Samson believes that *kol nidrei* provided a positive religious function. It affords the individual who had forgotten his vows a last-minute annulment before the beginning of Yom Kippur:

> If someone forgets that he had made a vow and didn't think to request an annulment from a sage, when he remembers he will specify it before a sage and he will be released. But the individual who does not remember [that he had undertaken a vow and needed to have it annulled], the prayer leader shall be his agent to express regret (*charatah*) on his behalf. Anyone who hears the prayer leader [chant *kol nidrei*], it is as if the prayer leader expresses regret on his behalf, and the vow is nullified by means of *charatah*.

Solomon attempts to justify the practice of *kol nidrei* by claiming that *kol nidrei* was itself a *charatah*. Of course the need to defend *kol nidrei* in this manner implies that some people were already questioning by the eleventh century whether *kol nidrei* was a valid procedure for the legal nullification of vows.

In addition, we learn from Solomon ben Samson that by the twelfth century some people were already claiming that if *Nedarim* 23b is *kol nidrei*'s talmudic source, then it must refer to future vows as well as past vows. Although Solomon personally doubted that *Nedarim* 23b was the halakhic source for *kol nidrei*, it was this very presumption that Rabbenu Tam would make the central basis for his emendation of *kol nidrei*.

---

3. Moshe Hershler, ed. *Siddur Rabbenu Shlomo* (Jerusalem, 1971), #101.

Whatever ethical and legal problems that would be raised in the next generation by Rabbenu Tam and others about kol nidrei, Solomon ben Samson apparently believes they were outweighed by the religious need to find a means of forgiveness for unfullfilled vows:

It seems to me that kol nidrei is said just prior to Yom Kippur because Yom Kippur is a day of atonement and forgiveness, and a day of teshuvah, and most of the world fails with regard to vows and oaths. . . .

At the same time, Solomon disapproves of the kol nidrei practice to say "As it is written in the Torah of Moses, Your servant" followed by:

The whole Israelite community and the stranger residing among them shall be forgiven, for it happened to the entire people through error (Numbers 15:26).

His objection is based on the fact that the context of Numbers 15:26 had nothing to do with the nullification of vows—indeed it refers to forgiveness for the sin of idolatry! Hence, it was inappropriate to suggest, by the phrase "as it is written," that Numbers 15:26 is a biblical proof text in support of the nullification of vows.

Solomon maintains that the correct practice is to omit "as it is written" and follow the recitation of kol nidrei directly with Numbers 15:26. He recounts that this practice was being followed in both the land of Israel and in Worms. Thus the Maharam's objection to the phrase "as it is written" (which was discussed in Chapter Four) was not new, and it was omitted by some communities long before the Maharam's thirteenth-century emendation.

The leaders in the fight against kol nidrei as a valid nullification of past vows were the twelfth-century French Tosaphists, Rabbenu Tam (Jacob ben Meir) and his father R. Meir ben Samuel. Rabbenu Tam argued that kol nidrei failed to meet any of the talmudic prerequisites for the legal nullification of vows:

It is forbidden for a person to release himself [from vows] without presenting a strong unconsidered circumstance (*charatah me'ikara*) before a single expert or three knowledgeable laymen. Moreover, the law is according to Rav Papa, the latest authority, who said in the talmudic tractate *Gittin* 35b that it is necessary to specify the vow.[4]

Rabbenu Tam marshaled three main precedents from talmudic tradition to make the case that *kol nidrei* cannot possibly be a legitimate nullification of past vows: (1) it is not presented before a sage or *bet din*, (2) it does not specify the vow, and (3) it fails to provide a *charatah*. It is also known from Asher ben Jehiel's subsequent rebuttal that Rabbenu Tam submitted yet a fourth point as well.[5] Since the *chazzan* nullifies his own vows as well as the vows of the community with his recitation of *kol nidrei*, the practice violates the principle in M. *Negaim* 2:5 that "a person cannot nullify his own vows."

At the same time, Rabbenu Tam also had to counter three points that suggested, despite all these problems, that *kol nidrei* had been clearly ordained by earlier authorities as a nullification of past vows. If *kol nidrei* is not a nullification for past vows, then (1) why is it written in the past tense, (2) why does it follow the practice for *hatarat nedarim* of being recited three times,[6] and (3) why does it include a biblical verse (Numbers 15:26) asking for God's forgiveness, if the vow never really takes effect?

Rabbenu Tam's answers to these points were recorded in the *Tosaphot* to *Nedarim* 23b, attributed to Moses of Evreux.[7] In response to the obvious argument that the language of *kol nidrei* is in the past

---

4. *Sefer haYashar* (Vienna, 1811; reprint ed. Shai Publications, 1959), #144.

5. See Rosh at *Yoma* 88b end, #28.

6. See n. 14 below.

7. Ephraim Urbach, *Ba'alei Tosephot* (Jerusalem: The Bialik Institute, 1955), 635.

tense, Rabbenu Tam maintained that key critical words such as *nedarna, ishteba'ena,* and *icharatna* could reasonably be construed as future-tense verbs. As for the fact that *kol nidrei* is recited three times, Rabbenu Tam cited *Menachot* 65a to the effect that all rabbinic declarations are supposed to be stated three times.

Finally, Rabbenu Tam claimed that *kol nidrei*'s request for divine forgiveness and atonement (Numbers 15:26) did not have anything to do with the sin of failing to fulfill past vows, i.e., vows already in force. Rabbenu Tam cited the precedent found in B. *Talmud Nazir* 23a and *Kiddushin* 81b, where a woman's vow to be a *nazir* was revoked by her husband without her knowledge. Despite her vow, the woman subsequently drank wine. Even though her vow had already been revoked by her husband, it was ruled that she required divine forgiveness and atonement because she believed her vow was still in force when she drank wine.

Rabbenu Tam claimed that this situation is analogous to *kol nidrei*. An individual recites *kol nidrei* at the beginning of the year, eventually forgets about it, then makes a vow and breaks it. Even though the vow has already been invalidated by *kol nidrei*, the individual considered the vow to be in effect when he or she violated it. The person requires divine forgiveness and atonement. Thus *kol nidrei*'s request for divine atonement and forgiveness of vows that technically never take effect makes perfect sense. *Kol nidrei* need not refer to unfulfilled past vows at all.

While Rabbenu Tam insisted that talmudic tradition made it impossible for *kol nidrei* to annul past vows, it was not his intent to eliminate the prayer. On the contrary, he sought to put *kol nidrei* on a sound legal footing. This was achieved by his recognition that talmudic tradition placed no such restrictions on *bitul tenai*, the anticipatory invalidation of future vows. The essence of his strategy was to identify *Nedarim* 23b as the talmudic source of *kol nidrei*. In so doing, Rabbenu Tam was able to argue that *kol nidrei* was never intended to nullify past vows. Its talmudic mandate was to invalidate future vows. It had been an error all along to phrase *kol nidrei* in the past tense:

Anyone who says "from the past Yom Kippur until the follow-ing Yom Kippur, may it come to us for good, regarding them all, we regret them" is simply making a mistake.[8]

The connection of *kol nidrei* with *Nedarim* 23b did not originate with Rabbenu Tam. It will be recalled that the eighth-century *Geonim* were already aware of it, though it is not clear whether they accepted the linkage. Similarly, in the eleventh century, Solomon ben Samson observed that many people considered *Nedarim* 23b to be the talmudic source of *kol nidrei*, though he himself doubted it. Rabbenu Tam's opinion became a watershed, not because it was new, but because he possessed the authority to take the bold step of emending *kol nidrei* to conform to its purported talmudic source:

> *Kol nidrei* which we say on Yom Kippur eve, my father emended to read "from this Yom Kippur until next Yom Kippur, may it come upon us for good; regarding them all, we regret them."[9]

However, at the same time that Rabbenu Tam affirmed the legitimacy of *kol nidrei* to invalidate future vows, he altered its legal status and thereby seriously circumscribed its applicability. As a retro-active nullification of past vows (*hatarat nedarim*), *kol nidrei* had pos-sessed, at least in the popular imagination, sweeping power to nullify all vows. But as an anticipatory invalidation of future vows, *kol nidrei* now assumed a restricted legal status and, thereby, limited powers of nullification. Rabbenu Tam ruled that *kol nidrei*, as a *bitul tenai*, per-tained only to vows people impose upon themselves (*nidrei atsmo*).[10] It had no authority whatsoever to nullify solemn promises made to others:

---

8. *Sefer haYashar*, #144.

9. Ibid.

10. An additional reason for restricting *kol nidrei*'s authority attributed to Rabbenu Tam is that the *kol nidrei* formula explicitly describes the vari-ous types of vows as being obligated "upon ourselves" (*al nafshatana*). See *Shibbolei haLeket, Hilkhot Yom haKippur*, #317.

[*Kol nidrei*] releases personal vows but for interpersonal vows, [such as] oaths made before a *bet din*, oaths made to a widow, and *mitzvah* obligations, it has no power. They do not depend upon one person's consent alone but upon the consent of God and the consent of the *bet din* [another manuscript adds: "upon the consent of the government"].[11]

Why did Rabbenu Tam consider it necessary to change *kol nidrei's* legal status? It is quite apparent that Rabbenu Tam's limitation of *kol nidrei's* authority to personal vows came in the context of a Jewish public that generally ascribed to *kol nidrei* sweeping powers to annul *all* interpersonal vows—even those made before a court, to the government, or in commercial transactions.

The twelfth-century Spanish *posek* Judah ben Barzillai, author of *Sefer ha'Ittim*, lamented that the common people were undertaking all sorts of vows and oaths, believing that *kol nidrei* had the power to get them off the hook, if necessary.[12] This picture of public perception is corroborated by Abraham ben Nathan of Lunel (Provence) in his early thirteenth-century work *Sefer haManhig*. He emphatically stressed that a *hatarat nedarim* has no power to nullify vows made to the government, before a court, or to one's fellow:

It is clear in the *Gemara* and among the *poskim* that *heter* (nullification) and *hafarah* (revocation) apply only to vows and oaths that a person vows or swears concerning oneself alone, such as eating or not eating, sleeping or not sleeping, and the like. But for what one person swears to another—and certainly to the government or a court—there is neither *heter* nor *hafarah* nor [even the possibility of] requesting annulment at all! The punishment of one who violates such vows will be very severe, God save him.[13]

---

11. *Sefer haYashar*, #144; cf. *Shibbolei haLeket*, #317.

12. Cited by Israel Davidson, "*Kol Nidre*," *American Jewish Yearbook* 25 (1923): 190.

13. *Sefer ha Manhig* (Jerusalem, 1967), *Hilkhot Yom Kippur*, #56.

Moses of Evreux clearly reveals that the power of *kol nidrei* to annul all interpersonal vows—including community ordinances and vows before a court—was a widespread, highly popular thirteenth-century belief shared by the folk and some rabbis alike:

> Since the early authorities thought, in error, that they could annul past vows, they used to say [in the *kol nidrei*], "Except for ordinances of the community and oaths of the *bet din*." But now, since we annul only future vows, we do not need to specify, "Except for ordinances of the community," for we annul only what a person vows to oneself, but matters between one person and another we are not able to nullify.[14]

In rebuttal, and to correct this public perception, some authorities specifically excluded such vows when *kol nidrei* was recited. Thus it appears that Rabbenu Tam's efforts to establish a restricted legal status for *kol nidrei* as a *bitul* and not as a *hatarah* constituted an effort to definitively convince the folk and even some rabbis that *kol nidrei* does not and *cannot* nullify interpersonal obligations. Despite these countermeasures, the French *posek* Jerucham ben Meshullam still found it necessary to complain during the fourteenth century that the common people, believing that *kol nidrei* spared them from punishment, were frequently perjuring themselves in court.[15]

Due to his stature and authority, Rabbenu Tam was able to win over the French and Provencal rabbinate, to the point where they

---

14. *Tosaphot* to *Nedarim* 23b. Rabbenu Tam similarly recounted: "I have heard that there are places where they say [*kol nidrei*] only once and this is correct. In their foolishness they became accustomed to saying it three times, as with an annulment of vows, and they included in ancient *machzorim*, 'Except for communal edicts and communal ordinances.' They imagine [*kol nidrei*] is an annulment of vows, but this is nonsense and it hovers in the air [i.e., there is no support for this assumption]. *Shibbolei haLeket, Seder Yom haKippurim*, #317.

15. Cited by Davidson, "*Kol Nidre*," 191.

accepted his emendation of the *kol nidrei* formula in the future tense. Rabbenu Tam's emendation was supported also by Abraham ben Azriel, the author of *Arugat haBosem*, and the Maharam—who added two emendations of his own.[16]

The Maharam (1215–1293) added a preamble to *kol nidrei*:

> By authority of the Heavenly Court, and by authority of the court on earth. With the consent of God and with the consent of the congregation, we hereby declare that it is permitted to pray with those who have transgressed.[17]

This preamble served not only as a special dispensation, allowing those excommunicated to pray on Yom Kippur with the community.[18] By citing the consent of the majority to justify the release of the congregation from its vows, it also functioned to strengthen *kol nidrei*'s legitimacy as a *hatarat nedarim* without fulfilling all of the talmudic requirements.

It is clear, however, from the discussion in Chapter Six, that the Maharam did not invent this preamble. The phrase "with the consent of X" was a common feature in exorcisms against demons and curses dating back to antiquity. The Maharam had reinstituted an ancient magical practice already associated with *kol nidrei* and endowed it with new meaning!

As discussed earlier in this chapter, the Maharam is also responsible for the omission of the phrase "as it is written in the Torah of Moses, Your servant" from the *kol nidrei* formula:

> After [the prayer leader] says *kol nidrei* three times, we do not say "as it's written in Your Torah," because the following verse

---

16. *Arugat haBosem*, ed. E. Urbach (Jerusalem: 1967), 476-477, 573.

17. *Teshuvot, Pesakim, uMinhagim shel Maharam*, ed. I. Z. Cahana, vol. 1 (Jerusalem: Mossad haRav Kook, 1957), #555; cf. *Tashbetz*, #134.

18. The Maharam's preamble fulfilled also a rabbinic teaching that sinners must be allowed to participate in prayer with the congregation on a fast day (B. T. *Keritot* 6b).

"they shall be forgiven" (Numbers 15:26) [is not a proof text for] the nullification of vows. Instead, we go directly to "they shall be forgiven," because [it has a proof text in] "God will forgive her" (Numbers 30:6), teaching that even one whose vows have been revoked requires atonement.[19]

The Maharam may have been addressing more than the omission of this phrase with this remark. By his citation of Numbers 30:6, the Maharam may have been refuting the argument put forward by critics of Rabbenu Tam's emendation that *kol nidrei* must refer to unfulfilled past vows or there would be no need for divine forgiveness. Numbers 30:6 explicitly states that God would forgive a woman whose father forbade her from fulfilling her vow. Consequently she must have required forgiveness, even though she was fully aware that her vow had already been revoked, demonstrating that divine forgiveness is required even for vows that never actually took force. Hence *kol nidrei* can request divine atonement without referring to past vows. The Maharam's proof text is actually superior to those brought by Rabbenu Tam, since there is no requirement for the vower to forget having said *kol nidrei*, or believe that the vow is still in force and to violate it while under that impression.

Both of the Maharam's emendations won universal acceptance throughout the Jewish world. Such was not the case for Rabbenu Tam. His emendation did not go unchallenged by the *poskim* of Germany, Italy, and Spain. Among the most prestigious *Rishonim* in this category were Eliezer ben Joel haLevi of Bonn (1140–1225), known as Ravyah; Isaiah ben Mali di Trani (1180–1250), known as the Rid; Asher ben Jehiel (1250–1327), known as the Rosh; and Nathan ben Judah, the early fourteenth-century German author of *Sefer haMaktim*.

The Ravyah retained the past-tense version of *kol nidrei*, citing the opinion of his contemporary, Raban (Eliezer ben Nathan of Mainz, 1090–1170), that "not everyone is knowledgeable enough to know

---

19. *Teshuvot, Pesakim, uMinhagim shel Maharam,* #555.

that one who vows is like one who builds an altar [for idolatry]."[20]
The Ravyah's defense of *kol nidrei* harks back to a theme that was
first encountered with Solomon ben Samson: an uneducated public
that is prone to making rash vows and failing to fulfill them must be
afforded some means of escaping divine punishment. That divine
forgiveness was of utmost concern was made clear in Ravyah's historical observation:

> In some countries the community says (*venislach*) in a loud voice
> so that the Holy One blessed be He will agree with their action
> and forgive every sin of His people Israel."[21]

The Ravyah insisted that *kol nidrei* fulfilled the necessary requirements for a legal nullification of vows. Like Solomon ben Samson,
he claimed that *kol nidrei* was a *charatah* expressed by the prayer leader
as proxy for all the people. At the same time, Ravyah went beyond
Solomon to assert that even though the prayer leader is not a sage,
he is accorded the power to release the congregation from its vows
by virtue of the consent of the majority.[22]

However, even as Ravyah supported the retention of the past-
tense version of *kol nidrei*, he too limited its power of annulment:

> But there is no need to say [in *kol nidrei*], "Except for commu-
> nal edicts and ordinances" since they have not consented to this
> nullification, nor does the individual sage have the power to
> release them [from communal vows].[23]

---

20. *Sefer Ravyah*, ed. Avigdor Aptowitzer, Part 2 (Jerusalem: Harry
Fischel Institute, 1964), *Masekhet Pesachim* 528. The identification of
idolatry with the act of vowing was not new with the Raban. He was em-
ploying a well-known talmudic critique of vowing found in B. T. *Nedarim*
22a.

21. Ibid.

22. Ibid.

23. Ibid.

The Ravyah's statement is very important, since it provides an instance of a rabbi who favored the traditional *kol nidrei*, but accepted Rabbenu Tam's limitation on the vows it had authority to annul. Similarly, Nathan ben Judah remarked in his defense of the past-tense version of *kol nidrei* that it annulled vows between "man and his Creator."[24] He too limited *kol nidrei* to vows that were left unfulfilled unintentionally or through unavoidable circumstance.

In his rejection of Rabbenu Tam's emendation, the Italian commentator Isaiah di Trani stressed that *kol nidrei* was an act of *teshuvah*.[25] Indeed, he claimed *kol nidrei* was recited precisely on Yom Kippur eve, because with *teshuvah* there is no transgression for which Yom Kippur cannot atone. Along the lines of the Ravyah and Solomon ben Samson, the Rid emphasized that *kol nidrei* should not be changed because it spared the public from punishment for the vows they failed to fulfill:

> The entire community releases one another and [*kol nidrei*] uproots the vow from its point of inception so that nothing will stand in the way of our atonement.

Like Nathan ben Judah, the Rid stressed that *kol nidrei* applied only to vows that had been broken inadvertently.

The most extensive rebuttal to Rabbenu Tam's emendation may be that of the Rosh:

> [Despite all of Rabbenu Tam's objections] it is clear from the custom of the early authorities, and proven by *kol nidrei*'s very language, that it applies to past vows that have already been transgressed, so that the people may be released and spared from punishment.[26]

---

24. Cited in *Orchot Chayyim, Hilkhot Yom haKippurim*, #29.
25. Cited in *Shibbolei haLeket, Seder Yom haKippurim*, #317.
26. Rosh to *Yoma* 88 end, #28; cf. *Piskei haRosh* to *Nedarim* 3:5 end.

The Rosh's refutation of Rabbenu Tam's argument is twofold. First, he asserts that the language of *kol nidrei* is indisputably in the past tense. In rebuttal to Rabbenu Tam's claim that the tense of some of the key terms were ambiguous, the Rosh cited the Hebrew *kol nidrei* recorded by Saadia. That text explicitly said "from the previous Yom Kippur until this Yom Kippur," and all the Hebrew verbs were clearly in the past tense.

Second, he believed it was the express intent of the early authorities that *kol nidrei* refer to past vows so that the public could be spared the serious divine punishment that would be incurred by the failure to fulfill vows already in force. The Rosh appears to be arguing that the public must not be deprived of the *kol nidrei* formula by which they could be released from a transgression that violated both a negative and positive biblical commandment: "He shall not break his word; he must carry out all that has crossed his lips" (Numbers 30:3). While Rabbenu Tam's emendation of *kol nidrei* afforded the public some relief by stopping future vows from ever taking effect, it did not address the far graver transgression of failing to fulfill vows already uttered and, consequently, already in force. From the Rosh's perspective, Rabbenu Tam's emendation would eliminate this vital protection.

As for the other legal objections raised by Rabbenu Tam, the Rosh sought to demonstrate in each case that *kol nidrei* fullfilled all the requirements of talmudic law for a valid nullification of past vows.[27] Regarding the objection that *kol nidrei* did not contain a *charatah*, he claimed the existence of a general assumption that anyone who failed to uphold a vow must have had a *charatah*. In addition, he maintained that the requirement for a *bet din* in the absence of a sage to authorize the release from vows was more than fulfilled by the fact that the entire congregation chants the *kol nidrei* in a whisper along with the prayer leader. Finally, the Rosh claimed that Rav Pappa's rule by which the vow must be specified before a sage referred only to situations in which the sage was concerned that the

---

27. Rosh to *Yoma* 88 end, #28.

vower wanted to annul a vow that involved a *mitzvah*. But since *kol nidrei* cannot annul *mitzvah* obligations, this rule does not pertain.

After having dispensed with the objections of Rabbenu Tam, the Rosh still had to deal with the fact that many Babylonian *Geonim* opposed *kol nidrei* on the grounds that it was incompatible with Rava's law that the anticipatory invalidation of vows should not be taught to the public. The Rosh claimed that the reason for Rava's opposition was his fear that the public would become reckless with their vows if they knew such a procedure existed. But the Rosh got around this objection, too, by arguing that his generation did not take their vows lightly.

In sum, the Rosh believed that *kol nidrei* was a completely valid retroactive nullification of vows. Like the Ravyah, the Rid, and Nathan ben Judah, he held that *kol nidrei* pertained only to vows that were made rashly or were unintentionally forgotten. At the same time, it is not totally clear whether the Rosh believed *kol nidrei* did in principle have the authority to nullify interpersonal vows.[28]

Surprisingly, a review of the *Tur* reveals that the Rosh's son, Jacob ben Asher (1270–1340), took no clear position on *kol nidrei*.[29] Without any expression of his own opinion, Jacob ben Asher provided a brief summary of the positions taken by Rabbenu Tam, the Rosh, and several *Geonim*. He recounts Rabbenu Tam's emendation of *kol nidrei* based on *Nedarim* 23b as its source, and explains how *kol nidrei* functioned as an anticipatory invalidation of future vows, its power limited, however, to personal vows (*nidrei atsmo*). To Rabbenu Tam's view, he appends those of his father, which are familiar: (1) *kol nidrei* was ordained by earlier authorities to annul past vows and to spare people from punishment, (2) it is recited three times because it is a valid nullification of vows, and (3) the verse *venishlach* appears in *kol nidrei* because atonement and forgiveness are required for vows that have been transgressed. Finally, he cites the negative opinions of Hai bar Nachshon, Natronai, and Saadia about *kol nidrei*. But when

---

28. *Korban Nitanel* to: Rosh to *Yoma* 88 end, #28 n. 70.
29. *Arba'ah Turim, Orach Chayyim, Hilkhot Yom Kippur*, #619.

all is said and done, Jacob ben Asher concludes only, "But the custom has already spread to say it everywhere."

Such a statement can hardly be described as an enthusiastic
defense of *kol nidrei*! Quite the contrary, it would suggest that Jacob
ben Asher may have been opposed to *kol nidrei*, but felt compelled to
support it anyway, perhaps in honor of his father. This conjecture is
supported by the *Tur*'s omission to clarify which *kol nidrei* version he
preferred, or to even debate the differences of opinion between Rabbenu Tam and the Rosh.

Notwithstanding the *Tur*'s statement that *kol nidrei* had become
a custom recited everywhere, the last word on *kol nidrei* had apparently not been said. For example, the fourteenth-century Spanish
commentator Isaac bar Sheshet (Ribash) maintained that *kol nidrei*
was confusing the public and should not be recited, with or without
Rabbenu Tam's emendation:

> Even if *kol nidrei* is changed to the future tense and it will func-
> tion as an advance stipulation (*tenai*), it is better not to say *kol*
> *nidrei* at all, so that they will not act irreverently with regard to
> vows . . . throughout Catalonia *kol nidrei* is not recited.[30]

Other sources give a similar impression that the fourteenth to
sixteenth centuries were a period of transition and ambivalence regarding attitudes about *kol nidrei*. Aaron ben Jacob HaKohen of Lunel
(Provence) preserves a *kol nidrei* version in his work *Orchot Chayyim*
(c. 1327) that is written totally in the future tense.[31] At the same
time, he remarks that *kol nidrei* was not said in some places. David
ben Joseph Abudarham, the Spanish author of *Sefer Abudarham*
(c. 1340), did not offer an opinion about *kol nidrei*, but instead quoted
the perspectives of Rabbenu Tam, the Rosh, and the *Geonim*.[32] Jo-

---

30. *She'alot uTeshuvot haRibash*, #394.

31. *Orchot Chayyim* (Jerusalem, 1956), *Hilkhot Yom haKippurim*, #29.

32. *Abudarham haShalem*, ed. S. A. Wertheimer (Jerusalem, 1963), 280-
281.

seph Karo's sixteenth-century *Shulchan Arukh* does not even raise *kol nidrei* as an issue. He merely wrote,"It is our custom to recite *kol nidrei*," and left it at that.[33]

However, by the late sixteenth/early seventeenth century a transformation had occurred. Rabbenu Tam's emendation had become a given. In his seventeenth-century commentary on the *Tur*, Joel Sirkes clearly states that *kol nidrei* is to be recited:

> According to the ordinance of Rabbenu Tam with the future [tense] and so have all the *acharonim* written.[34]

The sixteenth-century *posek* Mordechai Jaffe (1530–1612) of Prague, the renowned author of the *Levush*, boldly sought entirely to replace the traditional *kol nidrei* with a fully revised *kol nidrei* formula in the future tense. But despite all his efforts to win acceptance for his plan, he eventually conceded defeat:

> All of the language of *kol nidrei* that the *chazzanim* chant now is not precise and is in error. In the beginning it uses the singular and in the end it uses the plural . . . most of the content of *kol nidrei* that is printed in the prayer books has no substance nor any meaning except for the melody, and it is not known nor understood what's being said . . . how many times I tried to fix it and to teach the *chazzanim* what was correct but they were not able to change at the time of prayer because the customary melody was on their lips.[35]

For most of the *acharonim*, however, the debate had shifted to the issue of how to linguistically integrate Rabbenu Tam's emendation with the traditional *kol nidrei* formula. From their perspective, Rabbenu Tam's emendation could not simply displace the traditional

---

33. *Shulchan Arukh, Orach Chayyim, Hilkhot Yom haKippurim,* #619.
34. *Bayit Chadash* to *Tur, Orach Chayyim, Hilkhot Yom haKippurim,* #619.
35. *Sefer Levush, Orach Chayyim, Hilkhot Yom Kippur,* #619.

version of *kol nidrei*. Both opinions had to be upheld. A linguistic solution had to be found by which the public could fulfill its religious obligation according to both opinions.

In the seventeenth century, commentators began to issue rulings that called for various linguistic permutations of *kol nidrei*. The seventeenth-century commentator David ben Samuel haLevi (Taz) ruled that Rabbenu Tam's emendation should be accepted but without any further changes in the traditional text.[36] He was supported by Abraham Gombiner, the seventeenth-century author of *Magen Avraham*, another commentary on the *Shulchan Arukh*. But the eighteenth-century *posek* Jacob ben Tzvi Emden (Ya'abetz) insisted that both phrases, "from the past Yom Kippur" and "from this Yom Kippur," had to be recited.[37] However, in the nineteenth century, Israel Meir HaKohen (Chafetz Chayyim), the author of the *Mishnah Berurah*, held that the traditional phrase should be dropped in favor of Rabbenu Tam's emendation.[38]

Based on Rabbenu Tam's authority, most Ashkenazi *machzorim* in our own day have adopted his *kol nidrei* version. However, some Ashkenazi *machzorim*, following Emden, incorporate both phrases within the *kol nidrei* formula, with the traditional phrase for past vows most often appearing in brackets.[39]

Looking ahead, the medieval debate over *kol nidrei*'s legal authority to nullify vows will have profound repercussions in the modern period for the Jewish people's relationship with the Christian world and with *kol nidrei* itself. In addition, *kol nidrei* will continue to cause a rift between the laity and the rabbis.

---

36. *Turei Zahav* to *Shulchan Arukh*, *Orach Chayyim*, *Hilkhot Yom haKippurim*, #619.

37. Cited by Chaim Mordechai Margoliot, the nineteenth-century author of *Sha'arei Teshuvah*. See *Sha'arei Teshuvah* to *Shulchan Arukh*, *Orach Chayyim*, *Hilkhot Yom haKippurim*, #619; Nosson Scherman, *The Complete ArtScroll Machzor* (Brooklyn: Mesorah Publications, 1986), 61.

38. *Mishnah Berurah*, *Orach Chayyim*, *Hilkhot Yom haKippurim*, #619.

39. Kieval, "The Curious Case of *Kol Nidre*," 55.

10
The Music of *Kol Nidrei*

The Ashkenazi and Sephardi *kol nidrei* chants are essentially differ-ent melodies, with a few musical motives in common.[1] Idelsohn char-acterizes the Western and Oriental Sephardic *"kal nidrei"* chants as being based on *selichah* or *tefillah* modes.[2]

No single melody, the Askenazi *kol nidrei* chant is a concatena-tion of several melodic elements drawn from the musical corpus known as *Missinai* melodies.[3] The *Missinai* tunes consist of twelve short musical motives in a fixed or semi-fixed rhythmic pattern cre-ated by the Jews of the Rhineland (southern Germany and eastern France) in the eleventh to fifteenth centuries.[4] In turn, the *Missinai*

---

1. Personal communication from Cantor Phil Sherman.

2. A. Z. Idelsohn, "The Kol Nidre Tune," *Hebrew Union College Annual* 8–9 (1931–1932): 496. Some musical scores for Yemenite, Persian, Orien-tal Sephardic, and Moroccan *kol nidrei* versions (all of which are based on oral traditions notated in the twentieth century) can be found in Appen-dix II.

3. A. Z. Idelsohn, Th*esaurus of Hebrew Oriental Melodies*, vol. 7 (New York: Ktav, 1933), xxxiii–xxxiv; A. Z. Idelsohn, "The Kol Nidre Tune," *Hebrew Union College Annual* 8–9 (1931–1932): 497; Bathja Bayer, "Kol Nidre," in *Encyclopaedia Judaica*, 1972 ed.

4. Personal communication from Rabbi Geoffrey Goldberg. See A. Z. Idelsohn, *Thesaurus of Hebrew Oriental Melodies*, vol. 6 (New York: Ktav,

93

tunes were themselves derived from cantillation motives and German folksong (Minnesong).

These revered tunes were utilized at special liturgical occasions, particularly the *Yamim Noraim* and the *Shelosh Regalim*. Consequently the *Missinai* tunes appear not only in *kol nidrei* but permeate the entire High Holy Day liturgy. Some of the characteristic *kol nidrei* motives are also reflected in *Aleynu, Avot*, and *HaMelech*.[5] The *Missinai* tunes were only one part of Ashkenazic synagogue song that was developed between 900 and 1450 in eastern France and southwestern Germany. Idelsohn posited a reciprocal musical influence between Jews and Christians during this period, which fell into eclipse with the Crusades.[6]

Musicologists have speculated on the relationship between *kol nidrei* and western European music, but no consensus has been achieved. Cohen suggested that *kol nidrei* can be linked to early medieval Gregorian chant.[7] Idelsohn proposed that *kol nidrei* was mostly closely related to cantillation motives and German Minnesong.[8] Spector conjectures that the introductory motives of *kol nidrei* were based on the Babylonian Torah cantillation for *parashat Bereshit*.[9] Werner suggested that *kol nidrei* is "almost identical" with medieval *lais* (popular ballads).[10]

The musical history of *kol nidrei* is characterized by many variants, changes, additions, and embellishments. The earliest source on

---

1933), xxix–xxxvi; Hanoch Avineri, "Mi-Sinai Niggunim," in *Encyclopaedia Judaica*, 1972 ed.; Eric Werner, *A Voice Still Heard* (University Park, PA: The Pennsylvania State University Press, 1976), 26–35.

5. Werner (*A Voice Still Heard*, 37) has delineated eight motives that are shared by *kol nidrei* and other High Holy Day prayers.

6. Idelsohn, *Thesaurus of Hebrew Oriental Melodies*, vol. 6 (New York: Ktav, 1933), viii–xiv.

7. Francis Cohen, "Kol Nidre," in *The Jewish Encyclopedia*, 1916 ed.

8. Idelsohn, *Thesaurus*, vol. 6, xxix–xxxvi; *Thesaurus*, vol. 7, xxxiii–xxxiv.

9. Johanna Spector, "The Kol Nidre—At Least 1200 Years Old," *Jewish Music Notes* (October 1950): 3–4.

10. Werner, *A Voice Still Heard*, 26–28.

kol nidrei's cantorial development is the eleventh-century *Machzor Vitry* composed by Simcha ben Samuel:

> The first time he must utter it very softly like one who hesitates to enter the palace of the king to ask a gift of him whom he fears to approach. The second time he may speak somewhat louder. The third time more loudly still, as one who is accustomed to dwell at court and to approach his sovereign as a friend.[11]

As late as the fourteenth century, however, *kol nidrei* still did not have a set melody, but involved improvised chanting. Jacob ben Moses Mollin (1365–1427), also known as the Maharil, a principal authority on the synagogue worship of *Minhag Ashkenaz*, employed different melodies (*ya'arich bo biniggunim*) in order to extend the *kol nidrei* chant until nightfall so that latecomers would not miss it and so that everyone would have an opportunity to request pardon from his fellow.[12] The Maharil also chanted *kol nidrei* three times with increasing crescendo so that "we shall hear with awe and trembling."[13]

By the sixteenth century, however, it is presumed that *kol nidrei* had a fixed melody, selected from seven or eight of the *Missinai* tunes, which contains the basic stock of musical motives still utilized in the modern *kol nidrei*.[14] The existence of a fixed melody for *kol nidrei* has been inferred from the problems encountered by Mordechai Jaffe in his attempt to convert *kol nidrei* entirely into the future tense.[15] In Chapter Nine it was noted that the *chazzanim* would not accept the new words because they did not fit into a melody to which they were all accustomed:

---

11. *Machzor Vitry*, ed. Simon haLevi Hurwitz (Nuremberg, 1923), 388.

12. *Sefer Maharil* (Warsaw, 1802), *Hilkhot Leil Yom haKippurim*, 29.

13. Ibid.

14. Personal communication from Rabbi Geoffrey Goldberg; Werner, *A Voice Still Heard*, 37.

15. Werner, *A Voice Still Heard*, 35; Alfred Sendrey, *The Music of the Jews in the Diaspora* (New York: Thomas Yoseloff, 1970), 190–191; *Concise Encyclopedia of Jewish Music*, 1975 ed., s.v. "Kol Nidre."

How many times I tried to fix it and to teach the *chazzanim* what was correct but they were not able to change at the time of prayer because the customary melody was on their lips.[16]

In the eighteenth and nineteenth centuries *kol nidrei* underwent further development, marked by the beginning of divergencies between western and eastern European traditions. In western Europe the *chazzanim* incorporated into *kol nidrei* oratorical flourishes ("fantasias"), which were then in vogue in the west.[17] In eastern Europe, some of the *kol nidrei* motives were lost and replaced by new melodies. The *chazzanim* also included within *kol nidrei* the practice of vocalese (chanting without words).[18]

The first known musical notation of *kol nidrei* dates from the eighteenth century. It was included in a collection of synagogue songs (c. 1765) compiled by Aaron Beer, the premier cantor of his day in Berlin.[19] The opening theme of *kol nidrei* is recognizable in the sixth movement (bars 1–5) of Beethoven's C-sharp Minor Quartet (opus 131). *Kol nidrei* can also be heard in the C Major Symphony of Paul Dessau. Max Bruch composed in 1881 a concerto for cello and orchestra (opus 47) based on *kol nidrei*.[20] Arnold Schoenberg composed his "Kol Nidrei" (opus 39) in 1938 for speaker, chorus, and orchestra.

In the modern period, particularly in the relationship between *kol nidrei* and Reform Judaism, the *kol nidrei* melody would take on increasing significance. Jaffe's remarks to the effect that the meaning of *kol nidrei* inheres in its melody could not have been more prescient.

---

16. *Sefer Levush, Orach Chayyim, Hilkhot Yom Kippur*, #619.

17. Avineri, "Mi-Sinai Niggunim," 153.

18. Ibid.

19. The *kol nidrei* versions of Beer (1765), Naumbourg (1840–1874), Lewandowski (1871), and Abrahams Baer (1877) can be found in Appendix IV.

20. Bruch attributed his knowledge and interest in Jewish music to his friend, Cantor Abraham Jacob Lichtenstein (1806–1880) of Berlin.

11
Kol Nidrei
and Reform Judaism

Despite the protests of their *poskim*, the Jewish public in the Middle Ages commonly ascribed to *kol nidrei* the power to annul both vows to God and vows made to others—including vows made before a court or to the government. This assumption was not lost upon the Gentile European society in which the Jews lived. Considering the oath of a Jew to be untrustworthy, Christians compelled Jews throughout the Middle Ages to take a special Jewish oath (*More Judaico*) declaring that the oaths they swore in Christian courts would not be annulled by *kol nidrei* or by a Jewish court. To make matters worse:

> The oaths were accompanied by self-imposed curses, delineating the punishment, often in gruesome detail, if the testimony was falsely made; sometimes they were accompanied by humiliating rites, such as standing on a pigskin.[1]

---

1. Paul Mendes-Flohr and Jehuda Reinharz, eds., *The Jew in the Modern World: A Documentary History* (New York: Oxford University Press, 1980), 162 n. 13. The Jewish oath was not abolished in France until 1846. It was still administered in Rumania as late as 1904.

As late as 1844, a judge in Germany could force any Jew to go to the synagogue, don *tallit* and *tefillin*, and in the presence of the *Torah* swear that the oaths the individual made in court would not be annulled by *kol nidrei* or a Jewish court:

> There is many a state in Germany which still believes that the oath of a Jew is sacred only if it is sworn to the accompaniment of picayune ceremonies and it is done in the synagogue. The saddest situation of all exists in this respect in the Kingdom of Hanover. There, the Jew who swears an oath must put on *tefillin* and *tallit*. He must take the Torah scroll in his arm. He must assert that he will not have a Jewish court relieve him from the consequence of this oath, nor that the oath would be nullified through the *kol nidrei* prayer, nor that he looks upon Christians as idolaters.[2]

In response to the civil rights and equality promised by the 1812 Prussian edict of emancipation, "enlightened" Jews strove to acculturate within Gentile society and to conduct themselves as exemplary patriots.[3] They sought to raise Jewish prestige among their Gentile neighbors by transforming traditional Judaism into a modern and "enlightened" religion, founded upon eighteenth-century Enlightenment values of universal reason, ethics, and aesthetics.[4]

The Enlightenment had called for the elimination from religion of all irrational beliefs and superstitious customs so that the universal rational religion of all humankind could be revealed.[5] Under the

---

2. *Protocolle der ersten Rabbiner-Versammlung*, Brunswick, 1844. I am relying upon the English translation by Gunther Plaut, *The Rise of Reform Judaism* (New York: World Union for Progressive Judaism, 1963), 234–238.

3. Mendes-Flohr and Reinharz, *The Jew in the Modern World*, 140–144.

4. Robert M. Seltzer, *Jewish People, Jewish Thought: The Jewish Experience in History* (New York: Macmillan, 1980), 580–584.

5. Marc Lee Raphael, *Profiles in American Judaism* (New York: Harper & Row, 1984), pp. 3–9.

guise of reason, "enlightened" Jews satisfied their desire to do away with any Jewish practice that fostered prejudice against them or threatened their integration into non-Jewish society. Above all, "enlightened" Jews sought an end to historic Jewish isolation from Gentile society.

But as victims of prejudice often do, "enlightened" Jews believed they were responsible for their own suffering. This tendency toward self-blame was made perfectly clear at Israel Jacobson's (1768–1818) dedication of the first Reform temple in Seesen:

> Let us be honest, my brothers. Our ritual is still weighted down with religious customs which must be rightfully offensive to reason as well as to our Christian friends. It desecrates the holiness of our religion and dishonors the reasonable man to place too great a value upon such customs.[6]

In this context, "enlightened" Jews perceived *kol nidrei* as nothing short of a severe embarrassment and a principal cause of their suffering among the Gentiles. Misconceptions about *kol nidrei* by Jew and Gentile alike encouraged European society to think of Jews as unworthy of the civil rights and equality extended to them, and to consider Judaism as morally inferior to Christianity. Consequently, a movement arose for the abolition of *kol nidrei*. This effort was initiated not by the Reform rabbinate, but by a Reform laity composed of businessmen, intellectuals, and university-trained Jewish scholars.

Kol nidrei was omitted from the two prayer books utilized by the Reform Berlin *minyan* in 1815 and 1817.[7] It was also removed by the

---

6. Plaut, *The Rise of Reform Judaism*, 30.

7. Michael A. Meyer, *Response to Modernity* (New York: Oxford University Press, 1988), 49, 406 n. 145. The first prayer book was published anonymously. The second prayer book, *Die Deutsche Synagoge*, was edited by Eduard Kley and Carl Siegfried Gunsburg.

Hamburg Temple from its prayer books in 1819 and 1841.[8] *Kol nidrei* was abrogated by Isaac Noah Mannheimer in Vienna in the 1840s.[9] It was also left out of *Seder Ha-Tefillot—Forms of Prayer*, produced in London by David Woolf Marks and Hyman Hurvitz in 1841.[10]

But opposition to *kol nidrei* was not limited to Reform circles.[11] No less a figure than Samson Raphael Hirsch, the founder of modern Orthodoxy, eliminated *kol nidrei* from the Yom Kippur services held at Oldenburg in 1839.[12] Hirsch's motives for abolishing *kol nidrei* are not entirely clear. Immanuel Jakobovitz, a descendant of Hirsch, maintained in a 1963 letter to Petuchowski that Hirsch omitted *kol nidrei* as a temporary measure (*hora'at sha'ah*) due to dishonest business practices by some members of the Jewish community:[13]

> Hirsch in fact did omit *kol nidrei* once as a *hora'at sha'ah* in 1843, while in Emden (not Oldenburg), as a demonstration against the local acceptance of *kol nidrei* as an absolution from formal pledges and commitments.[14]

---

8. Jakob Petuchowski, *Prayerbook Reform in Europe* (New York: The World Union for Progressive Judaism, 1968), 337.

9. Meyer, *Response to Modernity*, 150.

10. Ibid., 174.

11. The elimination of *kol nidrei* was supported by Aaron Chorin (1766–1844), a famed talmudic scholar in Hungary.

12. Noah H. Rosenbloom, *Tradition in an Age of Reform* (Philadelphia: Jewish Publication Society, 1976), 69–70; Petuchowski, *Prayerbook Reform*, 337. Jakobovits maintained that Hirsch abrogated *kol nidrei* when he was rabbi in Emden, not Oldenburg. Petuchowski believes that Hirsch omitted *kol nidrei* in both places.

13. Rosenberg, *Tradition*, 420 n. 15.

14. Petuchowski, *Prayerbook Reform*, 337. Despite Jakobovits' family tradition that the elimination of *kol nidrei* was a one-time emergency measure, it should be noted that Hirsch omitted *kol nidrei* from a manual intended for all German Jews. Nor did he mention *kol nidrei*, *kapporot*, or *tashlikh* in his classic work *Horeb*. See Rosenbloom, *Tradition*, 69, 209.

The issue of how best to correct the problems created by *kol nidrei* and convince the German government to do away with the Jewish oath was the principal issue taken up by the 1844 Reform rabbinic conference held at Brunswick. Meyer contends that the Reform rabbinate convened the Brunswick conference in part to wrest control of the movement back from the Reform laity.[15] Samuel Holdheim proposed the issuance of a declaration that would correct the erroneous beliefs about *kol nidrei*:

> We recognize the accusations which have been made against us relative to the *kol nidrei*. To be sure they are unjust; but we must not fail to correct this impression with a relevant declaration.[16]

But Joseph Maier called for the abolition of *kol nidrei* itself:

> As far as the evils concerning the *kol nidrei* are concerned, the best way out would be to do away with the prayer altogether.[17]

The minutes of the conference tell us that Herxheimer, Formstecher, Herzfeld, and Frankfurter all agreed to the abolition of *kol nidrei*. Frankfurter was quoted as saying:

> As far as the *kol nidrei* is concerned, I agree with the many previous speakers. This so-called prayer has brought us so much unjustified defamation and so much misfortune that even its beautiful melody cannot compensate for it.[18]

The Brunswick conference concluded its deliberations with two declarations. With an eye toward abolishing the Jewish oath, the con-

---

15. Meyer, *Response to Modernity*, 131–132; personal communication from Dr. Lawrence A. Hoffman.

16. Plaut, *The Rise of Reform Judaim*, 235.

17. Ibid.

18. Ibid.

ference proclaimed that the oath of a Jew, undertaken in the name of God, was absolutely binding and required no further guarantees of any sort. In an apparent *quid pro quo*, the Reform rabbis also declared that *kol nidrei* was "inessential" and called upon the conference membership to work toward its removal from the following Yom Kippur service.

All sorts of alternatives were tried in an effort to find an adequate substitute for *kol nidrei*. Based on an ancient Palestinian custom, some congregations reintroduced the recitation of psalms (either 130 or 103) on Yom Kippur eve.[19] Other congregations adopted the hymn "O Day of God" ("O Tag des Herrn"), composed in 1840 by Leopold Stein (1810–1882) to the *kol nidrei* tune.

Some Reform rabbis composed entirely new Hebrew prayers in place of *kol nidrei*. While retaining the traditional melody and sometimes even the words *kol nidrei*, these prayers had little in common with the meaning of the original *kol nidrei*. The first to try his hand at such a prayer was Abraham Geiger, whose substitute for *kol nidrei* never once mentioned the word *vow*:

> All my transgressions, and the transgressions of this congregation, and the transgressions of all Thy people Israel—blot them out and make them to pass away from before Thine eyes; and purify our hearts from this Day of Atonement unto the next Day of Atonement, may it come to us for good. Our heart is broken, our spirit is humbled, we have no words. We rely on Thy love alone. O Merciful One, do not forsake us, for we are but dust. Requite us not according to our iniquities.[20]

It was not Geiger's prayer, however, but the 1870 Hanover version of *kol nidrei*, which became the standard substitute for *kol nidrei*

---

19. P. T. *Soferim* 19:2.

20. Petuchowski (*Prayerbook Reform*, 342). In the 1870 edition of his prayer book, Geiger dropped his own *kol nidrei* in favor of Stein's "O Day of the Lord."

in all European Liberal and Reform prayer books until 1929. This prayer does indeed mention "vows." But it has turned the original meaning of *kol nidrei* on its head, calling not for the annulment of vows, but for divine assistance in fulfilling them:

> (1) All the vows of the children of Israel which they vow unto Thee, O our King, to keep the words of Thy Torah and Thy testimonies, not to depart from the commandments either to the right or to the left, from this Day of Atonement unto the next Day of Atonement, may it come to us for good, yea, may all of them ascend and come and be accepted before Thee for mercy. And put it in their heart to love and to fear Thy great and awesome Name; and may they never be put to shame.

> (2) All the vows of the children of Israel which they vow unto Thee, O our Father, to walk in the ways of justice and loving-kindness and mercy, and not to harden their heart against their brothers, from this Day of Atonement unto the next Day of Atonement, may it come to us for good, yea, may all of them ascend and come and be accepted before Thee for mercy. And bend their inclination, and subdue their stiffneckedness, so that they may stretch out a hand to those who transgress against them. And may they be cleansed from their sin.

> (3) All the vows of the children of Israel which they vow unto Thee, O our Lord, lifting up their eyes unto Thee, O Thou that dwellest in the heavens, to return unto Thee with all their heart and with all their soul, from this Day of Atonement, may it come to us for good, yea, may all of them ascend and come and be accepted before Thee for mercy. And renew a steadfast spirit within them, that they may depart from their evil way, and not return unto their folly.[21]

All these replacements for *kol nidrei* demonstrate that the laity didn't much care about the message of the new prayer, as long as it

---

21. Ibid, 344.

was not morally objectionable and it could be chanted to the traditional *kol nidrei* melody. While the Reform laity and rabbinate objected to *kol nidrei*'s traditional message for the nullification of vows, the laity, in particular, had no intention of parting with *kol nidrei*'s traditional melody. In fact, the traditional Aramaic *kol nidrei* text was still chanted in many Reform congregations on Yom Kippur eve, despite its official elimination from the prayer book.[22]

The depth of nostalgic sentiment among the laity for the traditional *kol nidrei* melody is revealed in an anecdote about a dispute between Leopold Stein and his congregation over the substitute for *kol nidrei*. Although "O Day of God" was composed to the *kol nidrei* tune, that may not have been Stein's original intention. Philipson cites a 1907 article that appeared in the *Jewish Chronicle* in which Reverend Professor D. W. Marks of London

> [states] that Stein told him that when he wished to abolish the *kol nidrei*, his congregation was reluctant to dispense with the melody; he had therefore to promise that he would compose a poem which could be set to the same music.[23]

Although Reform rabbis in general were more concerned than the laity about the ideological content of prayer, this anecdote does not prove by any means that Reform rabbis considered the music to be insignificant or dispensable. Recall even the words of the Orthodox rabbi Mordechai Jaffe, who clearly recognized the music's power! In an addendum to his anthem Stein, too, acknowledged the power of the *kol nidrei* melody:

> This is not the place in which to deal with the value of the original *kol nidrei* formula, and to justify those—including the author

---

22. Meyer, *Response to Modernity*, 49–50, 321; Lawrence A. Hoffman, *Gates of Understanding Two* (New York: Central Conference of American Rabbis, 1984), 117.

23. David Philipson, *The Reform Movement in Judaism* (New York: Ktav, 1967), 459 n. 46.

—who have ordered its removal. That much, though, is certain, and cannot be denied by anyone: that the formula is by no means suited to introduce the holiest of all days, and that it would have been more suitable for any occasion but that of the eve of the exalted Day of Atonement. It almost seems that there has been an awareness of this incongruity. That is why, partly consciously, and partly unconsciously, a tune has been fitted to this uninspiring text—a tune which indeed did not fit the text, but which, to a high degree, was in consonance with the solemnity of the day it is meant to introduce. Whoever has once visited a synagogue on Atonement Eve will remember the deep devotion and the sincerity with which all those assembled listened to the first song of that evening. This most certainly cannot be ascribed to the uninspiring text, but solely and alone to the warm and pious spirit which breathes and lives in the tune.[24]

The precedent established by Reform in Germany was continued in America. None of the three classic Reform High Holy Day prayer books composed in America by Wise, Einhorn, or the Central Conference of American Rabbis contained *kol nidrei*.[25] Both Wise and Einhorn were classic universalistic rationalists, students of the Enlightenment, who were opposed to most of the highly particularistic Jewish rituals and folkways. The *Union Prayerbook* followed their precedents. Because of its problematic ethics, *kol nidrei* was probably particularly offensive to Wise and Einhorn. In 1883 Isaac Mayer Wise, in *The American Israelite*, specifically called for the abolition of *kol nidrei*:

> [It] has given rise to so many false accusations, and of which there is no mention in the Talmud, as it has no foothold whatever in the Bible. Sensible men ought to know that formu-

---

24. Petuchowski, *Prayerbook Reform*, 339.

25. Rabbi Leo Merzbacher also eliminated *kol nidrei* from his own 1855 prayer book *Seder Tefillah—The Order of Prayer for Divine Service.*

las of that kind are out of date and place, and ought to be dropped.[26]

The continued abrogation of *kol nidrei* by American Reform Judaism was also consonant with the 1885 Pittsburgh Platform, which rejected all ritual that failed to meet universal standards of reason and ethics:

> We recognize in the Mosaic legislation a system of training the Jewish people for its mission during its national life in Palestine, and today we accept as binding only the moral laws, and maintain only such ceremonies as elevate and sanctify our lives, but reject all such as are not adapted to the views and habits of modern civilization.[27]

Wise's *The Divine Service of American Israelites for the Day of Atonement* (1866), written in both English and German, began the service for Yom Kippur eve with a long "silent devotion" emphasizing the themes of personal stocktaking, God's beneficence, and divine compassion. This was followed by several stanzas from "O Day of God." Wise included only one of the traditional scriptural verses, Numhers 15:26 (*venislach*), printed in both Hebrew and German.

David Einhorn's *Olat Tamid* (1858), originally composed in German and translated into English by Emil Hirsch in 1896,[28] began the service for Yom Kippur eve with Psalm 84, followed by these verses:

> How lovely are thy tabernacles, O lord of hosts! My soul longs— ah, it faints—for the courts of the Lord; my heart and flesh shout

---

26. Cited by Joseph Heller, *Isaac M. Wise: His Life, Work, and Thought* (New York, 1965), 566.

27. Meyer, *Response to Modernity*, 387.

28. I have found an earlier English translation done in 1872.

to the living God. Even the sparrow finds a home, the swallow has a nest—where she shelters her brood. I repair to thy altars, O Lord of hosts, my King and my God. Lord of hosts, hear my prayer, and look down upon the countenance of thy children, who flock to thy courts, escaping from the tents of iniquity. Thou who art our sun, give us light and grace, that the repentant may walk in uprightness.

This text was followed by Stein's "O Day of God." Einhorn included the traditional scriptural passages (in Hebrew and English), but in a different order. Following the actual biblical chronology, he placed *selach-na* (Numbers 14:19) first, then *va-yomer* (Numbers 14: 20), and finally *nislach* (Numbers 15:26).[29]

The *Union Prayer Book Part Two* (*UPB II*; 1894), written in English, began the Yom Kippur evening service with a silent devotion that admitted transgression and sought divine pardon and human reconciliation. This was followed by a few stanzas of "O Day of the God," leading into Psalm 130, printed in Hebrew and English. This was followed by the three traditional scriptural verses also printed in Hebrew and English. Except for the addition of a new meditation in 1922, this format endured until the 1945 edition of *UPB II*.

By 1930, a new breeze began to blow in Reform Judaism. At the CCAR (Central Conference of American Rabbis) Conference of that year, a resolution was introduced to include an acceptable Hebrew *kol nidrei* version within the *Union Hymnal*.[30] The Conference transcripts reflect the struggle between continuity and change. Theodore Lewis (supported by A. W. Binder and Barnett Brickner) called for the inclusion of an acceptable *kol nidrei* text into the hymnal because nothing could touch *kol nidrei*'s emotional power:

29. The traditional order is (1) *venislach* (Numbers 15:26), (2) *selach-na* (Numbers 14:19), and (3) *va-yomer* (Numbers 14:20).

30. *CCAR Yearbook* 40 (1930): 101–103; Meyer, *Response to Modernity*, 321.

I thoroughly disagree with the theology expressed in the *kol nidrei* as every one of us does. However, in many of our congregations, *kol nidrei* is sung on Yom Kippur eve. *Kol nidrei* has a certain emotional force that no other song can convey to our people. Even in Orthodox synagogues they do not translate it and do not subscribe to its meaning, but use it out of pure sentiment.[31]

Other rabbis wanted to continue the practice of chanting "O Day of the Lord" to the traditional *kol nidrei* melody. David Philipson felt the original *kol nidrei* had caused the Jewish people too much suffering:

To me the *kol nidrei* brings to mind the picture of the enemies of my people throughout the ages and the persecution of your fathers and mine. . . . I am not going to permit my emotion and my love for the beautiful melody to blot out altogether my sense of history and of all which this meant to my ancestors on account of the misinterpretation which was placed upon the *kol nidrei*.[32]

Weis argued for the continued elimination of the traditional *kol nidrei* text from the hymnal. He did not object to the music of *kol nidrei* but to the ethical problems of its content:

. . . I feel that truth should not be sacrificed for art. However much the emotions may be touched, I think that the implications of Kol Nidre are such that we, the leaders of the congregations who know these implications, should not for the momentary satisfaction of the emotions allow the Kol Nidre to be used.[33]

The Conference empowered the Committee on Synagogue Music to include *kol nidrei* in the hymnal if a suitable version could

---

31. *CCAR Yearbook* 40 (1930): 102.
32. Ibid., 103.
33. Ibid.

be found. But the issue of *kol nidrei* surfaced again at the 1931 CCAR Conference.[34] Unable to agree upon an acceptable *kol nidrei* version, the committee called upon the Conference to decide what to do.

Apparently, the ante had been upped within the course of one year. Now some rabbis were proposing not just the restoration of an acceptable Hebrew *kol nidrei*, but the original Aramaic version. James Heller was particularly vociferous on this point, but a variety of rationales in favor of its restoration were put forth by Baron, Barnett Brickner, and Morris Clark.

Baron wanted the traditional *kol nidrei* text on sentimental, nostalgic grounds:

> It is entirely immaterial in this day whether there used to be any anti-Semitic menace on account of the presence of the original *kol nidrei* version. I feel this should be done on account of the historical and sentimental associations to be found in that version as well as in the music.[35]

Likewise, Brickner favored the traditional *kol nidrei* for its uncanny ability to create a mood of holiness and for

> the psychological value which it has in creating and stimulating a mood on the holiest day in the Jewish house of worship.[36]

Harry Ettelson represented the middle-ground position, arguing for the inclusion of a new acceptable version of *kol nidrei*:

> My feeling is that we ought to have the music in for the sentimental value of it; we ought to have it in with the best words available, but under no circumstances should we have words

---

34. CCAR *Yearbook* 41 (1931): 102–115.
35. Ibid., 105.
36. Ibid., 107.

that outrage our intellectual, our ethical and our spiritual view-
points.[37]

Samuel S. Cohon agreed with Ettelson and proposed his own
adaptation of the Hamburg *kol nidrei*, stressing the need for emotion
and drama in the services:

> The text here proposed expresses our sentiments and helps re-
> store a much-needed dramatic element to our Erev Yom Kippur
> service. We are erring in refusing to enrich our services with
> emotional content. . . . The finest setting of the "Day of God"
> cannot take the place of the *kol nidrei*.[38]

But those who objected to the traditional *kol nidrei*, a group represented by Philipson, Henry Berkowitz, Jonah Wise, H. G. Enelow,
and William Rosenblum, were not persuaded. Enelow summed up
their position:

> I earnestly hope that we shall not permit the folly against the
> ethical spirit of the Jewish religion by reintroducing into our
> liturgy on the most sacred evening of the year a formula the
> contents of which have formed a stumbling block to some of
> the most authentic interpreters of Judaism throughout the
> ages.[39]

In the end, the conference voted to include the traditional *kol
nidrei* melody in the hymnal without any words at all. Yet a seed had
been planted that would bear fruit in the years to come.

The first real cracks in Reform's extremely rationalistic ritual
emerged at the 1934 CCAR Conference. A group of four rabbis submitted a resolution noting "the many ideological and material changes

---

37. Ibid., 111.
38. Ibid., 113.
39. Ibid., 110.

in Jewish and general life which have taken place since [the Pitts-burgh Platform]" and called for a reevaluation of the Reform plat-form.[40]

Reform's reorientation was crystallized in the 1937 Columbus Platform. Its "Guiding Principles of Reform Judaism" backed away from the 1885 emphasis on universal rational religion. The Colum-bus Platform expressed a new appreciation and revaluation of ritual in religious life:

> Judaism as a way of life requires in addition to its moral and spiritual demands, the preservation of the Sabbath, festivals and Holy Days, the retention and development of such customs, symbols and ceremonies as possess inspirational value, the cul-tivation of distinctive forms of religious art and music and the use of Hebrew, together with the vernacular, in our worship and instruction.[41]

In consonance with the Columbus Platform, the CCAR Com-mittee on Ceremonies issued the traditional *kol nidrei* text in a one-page supplement to the *Union Prayerbook* that could be furnished to member congregations upon request.[42] In addition, the 1945 *UPB II* (known as the Newly Revised edition) contained several new ele-ments in the Yom Kippur eve service that had never before appeared. There was an introductory section that contained "Thoughts on Yom Kippur" and "The Rabbi's Prayer," followed by a few stanzas of "O Day of the Lord." The evening service proper began with "Light is sown for the righteous and gladness for the upright in heart" (Psalm 97:11). A new prayer was added calling upon God:

---

40. The rabbis were Barnett Brickner, Edward Israel, Iser Freund, and Isaac Landman.

41. Meyer, *Response to Modernity*, 391.

42. Personal communication from Rabbi Stanley Dreyfus. I have found in the HUC-JIR library a 1939 printing of the *UPB II* into which the tradi-tional *kol nidrei* text has been stapled.

Be near, we pray Thee, unto the grief-stricken and afflicted. Endow us with renewed courage to face our tasks unafraid, and strengthen us to do Thy will with perfect hearts.

This was followed by Psalm 130 and two of the traditional scriptural passages, *selach-na* and *va-yomer* (printed in Hebrew and English).

The traditional Aramaic *kol nidrei* text was briefly reinstated by the liturgy committee of the CCAR into the first printing of the 1945 *UPB II* and then removed from the market by its executive board.[43] This had nothing to do, however, with ideology. It seems that the CCAR liturgy committee had been in favor of chanting the traditional *kol nidrel* melody and was considering several alternative Hebrew texts for publication in the new prayer book.[44] President Solomon Freehoff explained at the 1944 CCAR Conference that a misunderstanding had occurred between himself and another member of the committee over what kind of *kol nidrei* text was to be included in the new prayer book:

> The record of the Liturgy Committee, as I had it and as Rabbi Marcuson, Secretary, had it, was to include the *Kol Nidrei* in the service. When the book appeared one member of the committee strongly objected. He claimed that the Liturgy Committee did not intend to include the traditional text but a re-written text. The matter was brought before the Executive Board and, after a long discussion, it was decided that we will not change the pagination of the books but will simply print the word Kol Nidre and omit the Hebrew text, while the rest of the pages will remain unchanged.[45]

---

43. Eric Friedland, "The Historical and Theological Development of the Non-Orthodox Prayerbooks in the United States" (Ph.D. diss., Brandeis University, 1967), 243–244.

44. Personal communication from Rabbi Stanley Dreyfus.

45. *CCAR Yearbook* 55 (1945): 33–34. Samuel S. Cohon was the member of the committee who had objected. The conference voted to sustain

In the compromise worked out by the executive committee, the traditional Aramaic text of *kol nidrei* was deleted from the second printing of the 1945 edition of *UPB II*. To avoid reprinting the entire book, the space taken by the *kol nidrei* text was replaced by an English prayer, the Hebrew words *kol nidrei*, and underneath them, in parentheses "the Kol Nidre Chant." This title was made intentionally vague in order to accommodate both those who now wanted to restore the traditional *kol nidrei* and those who still objected to it and preferred some other alternative.[46]

Like the 1870 Hanover prayer for Yom Kippur eve, the printed words of this English prayer delivered the diametrically opposite message from the unprinted words of the *kol nidrei* formula being chanted. The prayer called upon God to help the people fulfill their vows and lead them in the way of righteousness:

> All prayers which the children of Israel offer unto Thee, O our Father, that they may depart from sin, from guilt, and from wickedness, and follow the ways of Thy Torah, the ways of justice and of righteousness; yea, all the resolutions which we make from this Day of Atonement until the coming Day of Atonement—may they be acceptable before Thee, and may we be given strength to fulfil them. We have come to seek atonement and to ask Thy pardon and forgiveness. Turn us in full repentance unto Thee, and teach us to undo the wrongs which have been committed. Thus will Thy great and revered name be sanctified among us.[47]

Kol nidrei was finally reinstated by Reform Judaism in the 1978 edition of *Gates of Repentance*. The preamble established by Meir ben

---

the action of the Executive Board, but also moved and adopted that "the Conference prepare various Hebrew texts of the *Kol Nidre* to be furnished to members on request."

46. Personal communication from Rabbi Stanley Dreyfus.

47. This prayer is Cohon's English adaptation of the 1904 Hamburg *kol nidrei*. See Petuchowski, *Prayerbook Reform*, 346.

Baruch of Rothenberg was also restored. Calling for the fulfillment of vows, the preliminary paraphrase of *kol nidrei* echoes Cohon's English prayer, which replaced *kol nidrei* in *UPB II*. Most significantly, the English translation of *kol nidrei* itself, albeit free and far from complete, restored the theme of the annulment of vows:

> Let all our vows and oaths, all the promises we make and the obligations we incur to You, between this Yom Kippur and the next, be null and void should we, after honest effort, find ourselves unable to fulfill them. Then may we be absolved of them.[48]

This is followed by all three of the traditional scriptural passages (printed in Hebrew and English).

The restoration of the traditional *kol nidrei* text was born of a positive and proud attitude toward ritual, religious observance, and ethnic identity, an attitude that emerged in the 1960s and was given expression in the 1976 *Reform Judaism—A Centenary Perspective*:

> The past century has taught us that the claims made upon us may begin with our ethical obligations but they extend to many other aspects of Jewish living, including: creating a Jewish home centered on family devotion; lifelong study; private prayer and public worship; daily religious observance; keeping the Sabbath and the holy days; celebrating the major events of life; involvement with the synagogue and community; and other activities which promote the survival of the Jewish people and enhance its existence.[49]

---

48. *Gates of Repentance: The New Union Prayerbook for the Days of Awe*, ed. Chaim Stern (New York: Central Conference of American Rabbis, 1978), 252.

49. Meyer, *Response to Modernity*, 393.

IV
CONCLUSION

12
Summary of Findings

VOWS

Vows in the biblical and rabbinic periods operated on three levels—the social, the religious, and the magical. On the social level, vows were a common feature in the ordinary discourse and everyday speech of antiquity. People made vows at home, on the streets, and in business. Vows generally functioned in normal human affairs to enhance one party's credibility in the estimation of another. These vows were guaranteed by self-curses that took effect if the vower lied or otherwise failed to fulfill his or her obligation. All vows necessarily implied some risk to the life or property of the vower, a loved one, or a designated substitute. But folk religion constantly blurred the rabbis' distinctions between vows and oaths, between self-imposed obligations to God and solemn promises to others.

Vows played a prominent role in religious life as well. The most prominent vows in the Hebrew Bible are vows of dedication, which involved the dedication of an animal sacrifice or some other gift to God. Vows were pronounced at sacred sites such as temples or altars. It appears to have been customary to return to the site where the vow was made when the time came to fulfill it. Sometimes vows of dedication were an expression of thanksgiving for God's deliverance. But

117

at other times vows were expressed in an effort to win divine favor in times of trouble or special need. It was hoped that the acts of gift-giving and self-sacrifice implicit in dedicatory vows would motivate God to enter into a contractual arrangement to bestow kindness upon the vower.

But in addition to prayer and sacrifice, human beings fought back with magic against the exigencies of life. When it came to vows and oaths, folk religion constantly blurred the distinction between prayer and incantation, between the liturgical and the magical. Oaths and vows played a prominent role in the realm of therapeutic magic, functioning as one more countermeasure available to human beings in their attempts to ward off catastrophe. For example, to take an oath by the name of the deity was a well-known incantational for-mula, not a prayer but a magical spell, whose purpose was to compel the deity to perform a benefi-cent act or to make the swearer's words come true. In this manner the folk sought to guarantee the success or safety of various human endeavors.

Vows and oaths played a prominent role in the process of destructive magic as well. Believing in the magical power of words in general to influence reality, the practitioners of destructive magic took over the terminology and formulae for the creation of binding com-mitments and obligations in the human world and applied them to the satanic realm. Consequently vows and oaths became synonymous with curses and other types of hostile spells engendered by destruc-tive magic.

We now recognize a dynamic underlying vows and oaths that has heretofore been hidden from our view. The negative statements about oaths and vows expressed by some biblical and rabbinic sources reflect a twofold awareness. Not only did vows and oaths in normal human affairs necessarily imply curses that potentially jeopardized the life or property of the vower, but vows and oaths also belonged within the arsenal of curses engendered by destruc-tive magic that could be directed against the innocent individual at any time.

DEMONS

The ancients conceived of the world as filled with supernatural beings: gods, angels, demons, and spirits. Some demons were beneficent and revealed to human beings the decrees of heaven. Others were merely mischievous, but most were malevolent. Thousands of demons inhabited the air, palm trees, house roofs, and privies, and were the primary cause of both major disasters and daily inconveniences.

Vows, curses, blessings, and oaths attracted demons and other supernatural beings to carry out the content of the human utterance. Having set demons in motion, rash words could not be taken back. It was commonly accepted in antiquity that it was not God or the deities, but demons, who implemented the self-imposed curses activated by abused vows or oaths. When a person swore an oath, or when a magician conjured up a hostile vow, it was considered as if the demons had themselves simultaneously undertaken an oath to carry out the curses attached to them.

INCANTATIONS

Vows were not to be toyed with. They were a powerful weapon that could be manipulated by human beings to help or hurt other human beings. The individual needed protection not only from the demons activated by his or her own abused vows, but also from malevolent vows, i.e., curses, that had been directed by destructive magic against his or her person. In addition, the proliferation of demonic forces in the world could lead to national catastrophe because they might cause God to leave the Temple.

For these reasons it was very important to get rid of troublesome demons or, at least in some other way, to neutralize their power. The principal countermeasures against demons were incantations. Magical incantations presume that vows and oaths are as binding upon the world of demons as they are on human affairs. As a result, many

incantations are patterned after human models of obligation: nullifi-
cations of vows, writs of divorce, and contracts. Just as one party can
compel another to provide testimony under oath in a human court
of law, so, too, incantations work by forcing demons to swear vows
or oaths. Exorcisms, for example, have the power to bind and compel demons to undertake oaths of banishment and exile. By compelling demons to swear an oath or vow via special formulae, magical
incantations bound the will of demons, angels, and other supernatural
beings to perform human bidding.

THE NULLIFICATION OF VOWS

Biblical sources made it abundantly clear that vows were a serious
business that must be carried out. At the same time, however, Numbers 30 established the principle of the revocation of vows (*hafarat
nedarim*) for female minors and married women. Fathers had the
power to revoke the vows of their daughters (as minors), and husbands had the power to revoke the vows of their wives. Since no other
population besides female minors and married women has even the
possibility of being released from their vows, biblical sources encouraged people not to make vows at all. Numbers 30 nowhere mentions
the nullification of vows (*hatarat nedarim*). Indeed, there is no provision for the nullification of vows in the Hebrew Bible. It is strictly a
postbiblical phenomenon.

Despite the absence of a biblical precedent for the nullification
of vows, a procedure to annul vows does exist in rabbinic tradition.
Vows can be annulled solely by a sage or a *bet din* composed of three
knowledgeable laymen. Based on Numbers 30, the rabbis drew a
serious philosophical and legal distinction between the revocation of
vows (*hafarat nedarim*) and the nullification of vows (*hatarat nedarim*):
fathers and husbands alone possessed the authority to revoke, respectively, the existing vows of their daughters (as minors) and wives. In
contrast, neither the sage nor the *bet din* held the authority to revoke
vows already in force (*hafarat nedarim*). Instead, the sages resorted

to a legal fiction based on the concept of *charatah* (regret). It was the task of the sage or *bet din* to find a *petach*, strong grounds, upon which the vower would have truly regretted having made his vow. Since the vow was made by mistake and did not reflect the vower's true intent, the sage or *bet din* released the individual from his or her vow. In modern parlance, we would designate this process as "finding a legal loophole." By means of a second legal fiction consisting in the vow's retroactive nullification *ab initio*, at the moment of its inception (partially effected through the threefold declaration of *mutar lecha*), the vow was rendered by the sage or *bet din* as if it no longer existed and never had existed. Consequently it was as if the vow had never taken force.

Jewish law also recognizes a procedure for the anticipatory invalidation of vows that may be undertaken in the future. This action prevents future vows from ever taking force. This procedure involves the declaration of intent to invalidate future vows in the form of an advance stipulation (*bitul tenai*). This procedure is described in B. T. *Nedarim* 23b. Rava did not want this procedure to be taught to the public, lest they begin to disregard their vows. Rava's objections notwithstanding, by the eighth century *Nedarim* 23b was attributed to be the talmudic source of *kol nidrei*.

VERSIONS OF *KOL NIDREI*

The author of *kol nidrei* and its exact date of origin are unknown. The earliest known version of *kol nidrei* was preserved in the ninth-century prayer book *Seder Rav Amram*. Given our knowledge of the talmudic procedure and terminology for the nullification of vows, we now recognize that this *kol nidrei* version constituted a retroactive nullification of vows *ab initio*. This *kol nidrei* provides a blanket nullification of vows, even if the vows were intentionally violated. God appears to play almost no active role in Rav Amram's *kol nidrei*. The people arrogate to themselves the authority to nullify their vows. God's pardon and forgiveness are invoked at the end. This *kol nidrei* formula also included a blessing for the nullification of vows, which was still being practiced as late as the thirteenth century.

An Aramaic version of *kol nidrei* was composed by Hai bar Sherira in the tenth or eleventh century and included in his prayer book, which has been lost. This *kol nidrei* is not a nullification of vows but a prayer for divine absolution. Not only is Hai Gaon's *kol nidrei* permeated with the language of penitential prayer, but it quite explicitly expresses the view that it is up to God to forgive the people and to release them from their vows. Hai Gaon's version of *kol nidrei* also limited the nullification of vows to only those vows that went unfulfilled due to unintentional neglect or unavoidable circumstances.

In the twelfth century, Rabbenu Tam converted *kol nidrei* to refer to future vows. His emendation was eventually accepted by most *Ashkenazim*. It was never accepted by Western *Sephardim*. Oriental *Sephardim* combined both the traditional *kol nidrei* version and Rabbenu Tam's emendation. All three *kol nidrei* versions straddle the fence between Amram's nullification of vows and Hai's prayer for absolution, by combining elements of both in equal measure. Yet the classic Ashkenazi and Western Sephardi *kol nidrei* surprisingly lack one element necessary for a prayer of absolution: they never mention God! At the same time, both the Western and Oriental Sephardi *kol nidrei* lack a critical element associated with the nullification of vows: they never mention the terminology of legal fiction.

KOL NIDREI AND INCANTATION TEXTS

Demonology held a significant place in the life of Babylonian Jewry during the talmudic period. Indeed, Jewish demonology flourished in the cultural climate of Babylonia, where Persian dualism and the belief in demons were widespread. Having a reputation for their magical skills, Babylonian Jews employed a variety of countermeasures to protect themselves from demons: the study of Torah, the fulfillment of commandments, incantations, amulets, prayer, and magic bowls.

Jewish demonology is known principally through the study of the Babylonian Talmud. Since 1853, however, more than 100 magical incantations inscribed on earthenware bowls were discovered in Babylonia, principally at Nippur, but also at other sites in the Middle East. Dating from the fourth to seventh century C.E., these incantation texts were roughly contemporaneous with the formation of the Talmud. They were written primarily in Aramaic, Mandaic, and Syriac.

The discovery of the Babylonian magic bowls sheds new light on the religious praxis of Babylonian Jewry, particularly with respect to *kol nidrei*. For example, some of the incantation texts inscribed on the magic bowls nullified the malevolent oaths, curses, and spells. In addition, some of these incantations employed terms found in *kol nidrei*, including, remarkably, the very words "*kol nidrei*."

The linguistic parallels and conceptual affinities between *kol nidrei* and the Babylonian incantation texts have been interpreted in two ways. The minimal claim, represented by Levine, holds that *kol nidrei* was a legal fiction for the nullification of human vows. Believing in the power of legal formulae such as the nullification of vows, bills of divorce, and contracts to bind humans and demons alike, the authors of these Babylonian incantation texts utilized the same legal terminology as found in *kol nidrei* but applied it to a magical context.

The maximal claim, represented by Gordon and Gold, holds that *kol nidrei* was a magical incantation in its own right and can best be understood as belonging within the context of the Babylonian incantation texts. As Neusner points out, Nippur, the archeological site where many of the magical bowls were found, was "just down the road" from Sura, the site of a major Geonic academy. In this view *kol nidrei* did not annul human vows at all. *Kol nidrei* functioned as an incantation against demons by annulling the entire range of curses people bring upon themselves and others.

Like various incantation texts, other unknown *kol nidrei* versions may also have included actual language for nullifying the vows undertaken by (i.e., imposed upon) the demons themselves. The purpose of *kol nidrei* was to protect human beings from the harm of demons during the particularly vulnerable time of Yom Kippur, the Day of Judgment. *Kol nidrei* may have been chanted in tandem with a *hatarat nedarim* for human vows.

KOL NIDREI'S PLACE OF ORIGIN

It should be stated at the outset that the process of tracing lines of cultural transmission is a risky business. It is frequently the case that little can be said with much certainty. Early twentieth-century scholarship tended toward the conclusion that *kol nidrei* was originally a Palestinian custom that subsequently won widespread popularity in Babylonia. But no definitive proof exists to warrant such a conclusion at this time. Instead there is a growing body of evidence to cast doubt on the conventional understanding that *kol nidrei* was of Palestinian origin. Based upon the linguistic and conceptual parallels between *kol nidrei* and the Babylonian magic bowl incantations, current scholarship presumes that *kol nidrei* originated in Babylonia.

KOL NIDREI AND THE BABYLONIN *GEONIM*

In the eighth century many of the Babylonian *Geonim* prohibited the nullification of vows. This stance was not monolithic. Some *Geonim* permitted *hatarat nedarim*. Both Yehudai and Hai bar Nachshon conceded that some *Geonim* did in fact practice *ha'aramot* (legal fictions) and *charatot* on Yom Kippur eve.

The Babylonian *Geonim* were far from united with regard to *kol nidrei* as well. Natronai, Amram, and Hai bar Nachshon condemned the recitation of *kol nidrei*; Saadia permitted it under specific circumstances; Hai bar Sherira approved only his own version of *kol nidrei*; Paltoi may have permitted it outright. In addition to these data, sources in both *Sha'arei Teshuvah* and *Shibbolei haLeket* claim that other unnamed *Geonim* favored *kol nidrei*.

The Babylonian *Geonim* were certainly aware of *kol nidrei*'s popularity in folk religion as an incantation against demons. Yet, except for the brief remark of Rav Amram, the *Geonim* uniformly declined to refer to *kol nidrei* as a magical incantation. They described *kol nidrei* as a nullification of human vows and expressed their approval or disapproval of it on legal grounds.

Several scholars have sought to find deeper reasons to account for the Geonic attitude toward *kol nidrei*. Kieval contends that the *Geonim* were prepared to accept *kol nidrei* as a prayer for divine absolution but not as a nullification of vows. Both Mann and Baron describe the Geonic attitude toward *kol nidrei* as impacted by various pressure groups who either opposed the practice of nullifying vows (the Karaites) or clamored for it (the folk). But all these opinions take the Geonic opposition to *kol nidrei* on legal grounds at face value. They do not really provide a "deeper" understanding at all.

In contrast, Gordon and Deshen propose that the underlying reason for Geonic rejection of *kol nidrei* was their opposition to its utilization as an incantation against demons. We have revised this hypothesis to speculate that the *Geonim* did not oppose the private use of magical incantations in general, but specifically objected in this instance to the introduction of a magical incantation into public synagogue worship, particularly on Yom Kippur. The official Geonic opposition on legal grounds may have been a clever strategy by which the *Geonim* won public support for their position but still avoided a clash with the folk over the appropriate place of magic in religion.

However, when all is said and done, this scenario can be nothing more than a matter of speculation. For the Geonic sources uniformly attributed their opposition to *kol nidrei* to legal grounds. Beyond this, the Geonic sources do not go.

KOL NIDREI IN THE MEDIEVAL PERIOD

By the advent of the Middle Ages, *kol nidrei* had already become a hallowed folk custom among most of the Jewish world, even though, by the eleventh century, some rabbis had begun to question the validity of *kol nidrei* as a nullification of past vows.

The leaders in the fight against *kol nidrei* as a legitimate nullification of past vows were the twelfth-century French Tosaphists, Rabbenu Tam (Jacob ben Meir) and his father Meir ben Samuel. Rabbenu Tam argued that *kol nidrei* failed to meet any of the talmudic requirements for the legal nullification of past vows: (1) it is not recited by a sage or *bet din*; (2) it does not specify the vow; (3) it fails to provide a *charatah*; and (4) it violates the rule that a person cannot nullify his own vow.

But it was not Rabbenu Tam's intention to eliminate *kol nidrei*. Quite the contrary: Rabbenu Tam sought to put *kol nidrei* on a sound legal footing. Although *kol nidrei* failed to meet the talmudic prerequisites for the nullification of past vows, Rabbenu Tam recognized that talmudic tradition placed no such restrictions on *bitul tenai*, the anticipatory invalidation of future vows described in B. T. *Nedarim* 23b. By identifying B. T. *Nedarim* 23b as the talmudic source of *kol nidrei*, Rabbenu Tam argued that *kol nidrei* had never been intended to nullify past vows. He claimed its talmudic mandate was to invalidate future vows and that it had been a mistake to phrase *kol nidrei* in the past tense.

At the same time that Rabbenu Tam affirmed the legitimacy of *kol nidrei* to invalidate future vows, he altered its legal status and thereby circumscribed its powers of nullification. As a retroactive nullification of past vows (*hatarat nedarim*), *kol nidrei* had possessed, at least in the popular imagination, sweeping authority to nullify all vows. But as an anticipatory invalidation of future vows, *kol nidrei* now assumed a restricted legal status and, thereby, lesser powers of nullification. As a *bitul tenai*, Rabbenu Tam ruled that *kol nidrei* pertained only to vows that people impose upon themselves (*nidrei atzmo*), but had no authority whatsoever to nullify interpersonal vows, such as those taken before a court or the government.

It is apparent that Rabbenu Tam's limitation of *kol nidrei*'s authority to personal vows came in the context of a Jewish public that generally ascribed to *kol nidrei* sweeping powers to annul all vows—

including vows made before a court, to the government, and in commercial transactions. The absolute authority of *kol nidrei* in the public imagination is substantiated by the vigorous statements made by Judah ben Barzillai, Abraham ben Nathan of Lunel, the Ravyah, Nathan ben Judah, and Jerucham ben Meshullam, denying that *kol nidrei* has any power to annul vows beyond those made with God or imposed upon oneself.

That *kol nidrei* was considered even by some rabbis to have absolute power is confirmed by the reports of Moses of Evreux and Rabbenu Tam that some rabbinic authorities specifically excluded communal vows and vows made before a court in the recitation of *kol nidrei* itself. Thus it appears that Rabbenu Tam's efforts to establish a restricted legal status for *kol nidrei* as a *bitul* and not as a *hatarah* constituted an effort to convince the folk and even some rabbis that *kol nidrei* does not and *cannot* nullify interpersonal obligations. The fact that both the Ravyah and Nathan ben Judah also supported the past-tense version of *kol nidrei* suggests that while the *poskim* may have differed among themselves about Rabbenu Tam's emendation, many of them were united in opposing the public perception that *kol nidrei* had the power to annul anything more than personal vows.

Due to his stature and authority, Rabbenu Tam was able to win over the French and Provencal rabbinate to the point where they accepted his emendation of the *kol nidrei* formula in the future tense. But Rabbenu Tam's emendation did not go unchallenged by the *poskim* of Germany, Italy, and Spain. Among the most prestigious opponents of Rabbenu Tam's emendation were the Ravyah, the Rid, and the Rosh. Harking back to a theme first enunciated by Solomon ben Samson, all three *Rishonim* defended the retention of the past-tense version of *kol nidrei* because it afforded the public protection from serious divine punishment they would otherwise incur for their failure to fulfill vows already in force.

As for the other legal objections raised by Rabbenu Tam, these *poskim* sought to demonstrate in each case that *kol nidrei* fulfilled all the requirements of talmudic law for a valid nullification of past vows. The Ravyah, like Solomon ben Samson, maintained that *kol nidrei* was itself a *charatah*. He also argued that the prayer leader, though he is not a sage, may release the congregation from its vows by virtue of the consent of the majority. Along the same lines, the Rosh claimed that the requirement for a *bet din* in the absence of a sage to authorize the release from vows was more than fulfilled by the fact that the entire congregation chants the *kol nidrei* along with the prayer leader. In addition, the Rosh maintained that it was not the prayer leader who released his own vows but the congregation who released him. Finally, the Rosh insisted that Rav Papa's rule about specifying the vow pertained only to situations in which the sage was concerned that the vower wanted to annul a vow that involved a *mitzvah*, and that *kol nidrei* does not involve such vows.

By the end of the thirteenth century, *kol nidrei* had undergone another major emendation. Meir ben Baruch of Rothenberg (Maharam) added a preamble to *kol nidrei* that won widespread acceptance throughout the Jewish world. The Maharam's emendation served not only as a special dispensation, allowing those excommunicated to pray on Yom Kippur with the community; by justifying the release of the congregation from its vows upon the consent of the majority, it also functioned to strengthen the legitimacy of *kol nidrei* as a nullification of vows. Believing that the phrase "as it is written in the Torah of Moses, Your servant" conveys the erroneous impression that Numbers 15:26 is a biblical proof text for the nullification of vows, the Maharam also omitted it from *kol nidrei*.

A review of the opinions of several commentators between the fourteenth and sixteenth centuries reflects a period of transition in attitudes about *kol nidrei*. The *Tur*, for example, deals with *kol nidrei* in a very ambiguous manner: Jacob ben Asher does not debate the differences of opinion between Rabbenu Tam and his father; nor does he express which *kol nidrei* version he preferred. Other fourteenth-century commentators reflect a similar ambivalence over what to do with *kol nidrei*. Aaron ben Jacob haKohen of Lunel preserves a *kol nidrei* version in his work *Orchot Chayyim* that is written totally in the future tense. At the same time, he remarks that *kol nidrei* is said in some places. The Spanish commentator Isaac bar Sheshet (Ribash) argues that kol nidrei confuses the public, so it should not be recited, with or without Rabbenu Tam's emendation. David ben Joseph Abudarham reviews various sources but offers no opinion of his own. Joseph Karo's sixteenth-century Shulchan Arukh ambiguously states, "It is our practice to recite kol nidrei," and leaves it at that.

By the late sixteenth/early seventeenth century, however, a transformation had occurred. Rabbenu Tam's emendation had become a given. In his commentary Bayit Chadash, Joel Sirkes clearly states that kol nidrei is to be recited according to the version of Rabbenu Tam and that this is the opinion of "all the acharonim." Mordechai Jaffe, the author of the Levush, boldly seeks to convert the kol nidrei formula entirely into the future tense.

But most of the acharonim sought to find a way to integrate Rabbenu Tam's emendation with the traditional kol nidrei text, so that a person could fulfill one's religious obligation according to both opinions. In the seventeenth century, commentators began to issue rulings that called for various linguistic permutations of kol nidrei. The seventeenth-century commentator David ben Samuel haLevi (Taz) ruled that Rabbenu Tam's emendation should be accepted but without any further changes in the traditional text. He was supported by Abraham Gombiner, the seventeenth-century author of Magen Avraham, another commentary on the Shulchan Arukh. But the eighteenth-century posek Jacob ben Tzvi Emden (Ya'abetz) insisted that both phrases, "from the past Yom Kippur" and "from this Yom Kippur," had to be recited. However, in the nineteenth century, Israel Meir HaKohen (Chafetz Chayyim), the author of the Mishnah Berurah, held that the traditional phrase should be dropped in favor of Rabbenu Tam's emendation.

Based on Rabbenu Tam's authority, most Ashkenazi machzorim in our own day have adopted his kol nidrei version. However, some Ashkenazi machzorim, following Emden, incorporate both phrases within the kol nidrei formula, with the traditional phrase for past vows most often appearing in brackets.

THE MUSIC OF *KOL NIDREI*

The Ashkenazi and Sephardi *kol nidrei* chants are essentially different melodies, with a few musical motives in common. The Ashkenazi *kol nidrei* is a series of seven or eight short musical motives, known as *Missinai* melodies, that were created by the Jews of southern Germany and eastern France in the eleventh to fifteenth centuries. *Kol nidrei* is most closely related to and derives from a combination of cantillation motives and German folksong.

The musical history of *kol nidrei* is characterized by many variants, changes, additions, and embellishments. The basic stock of musical motives that have come to characterize the modern *kol nidrei* were essentially fixed in the sixteenth century.

The practice of chanting *kol nidrei* three times with an increasing crescendo goes as far back as the eleventh century. Originally, the threefold repetition was a sign of *kol nidrei*'s status as a *hatarat nedarim*. But the Maharil practiced it so that everyone would have a chance to request pardon from one's fellow before Yom Kippur began, to create a mood of awe, and so that latecomers would not miss the *kol nidrei* chant. For *kol nidrei* to be a valid nullification of vows, many *poskim* ruled that *kol nidrei* needed to be chanted or whispered by the entire congregation in unison.

KOL NIDREI AND REFORM JUDAISM

Viewing *kol nidrei* as the motivating force behind the humiliating Jewish oath and as a threat to their newly won acceptance within Gentile society, some Reform Jews and even a few Orthodox rabbis began to omit *kol nidrei* in 1817. Initially, the anti-*kol nidrei* movement within Reform was led by the laity. The Reform rabbinate officially abrogated *kol nidrei* at the 1844 Brunswick conference.

In spite of all the creative alternatives for *kol nidrei*, a powerful segment among the Reform community was unwilling to part with *kol nidrei*'s traditional melody. More research is required to determine how widespread this attitude was among the laity and the rabbinate, and whether a significant contrast exists between them. But we do know that the laity, in particular, did not much care about the message of the new prayer, as long as it was morally edifying and it could be chanted to the traditional *kol nidrei* melody. Like Mordechai Jaffe in the sixteenth century, the nineteenth-century anti-*kol nidrei* forces failed to differentiate between the *kol nidrei* text and its melody, with the result that they underestimated the popularity of the latter.

The precedent established by Reform in Germany was brought to America by the wave of German immigrants in the late nineteenth century. Neither Wise, Einhorn, nor the CCAR included *kol nidrei* in their High Holy Day prayer books, published in 1866, 1896, and 1894, respectively. *Kol nidrei* failed to meet the standards of ritual laid down by the universal rational religion as enunciated in the 1885 Pittsburgh Platform.

The Reform stance toward *kol nidrei* slowly began to shift around 1930 in tandem with changes in Reform ideology. The new breeze began to blow at the 1930 and 1931 CCAR conferences, with some rabbis calling for the restoration of an acceptable Hebrew *kol nidrei*, even the traditional Aramaic version, into the *Union Hymnal*. Although the conference decided to publish the *kol nidrei* melody in the hymnal without any words at all, a page had been turned in the history of the relationship between Reform Judaism and *kol nidrei*. The promulgation of the 1937 Columbus Platform signaled Reform ideology's backing away from its overwhelming emphasis on rational religion and its readiness to extend a new sympathetic hearing to Jewish ritual. *Kol nidrei* was eliminated from *The Union Prayerbook* from 1894 to 1978, except for its brief reinstatement, by error, in the short-lived original printing of the 1945 *UPB II*. But regardless of its omission from *UPB II*, and in consonance with the pattern established in Germany, the traditional *kol nidrei* text was still being chanted on Yom Kippur eve in some Reform congregations by 1930 at the latest, and probably much earlier.

This was certainly the case by 1945, when the Hebrew words "*kol nidrei*" and "the *kol nidrei* chant" appeared for the first time in the 1945 *UPB II*. Accompanying the *kol nidrei* chant was an English translation that followed the 1904 Hamburg prayer, in calling not for the nullification of vows but for their fulfillment.

Kol nidrei was officially reinstated by the Reform movement in the *Gates of Repentance* (1978). Not only was the traditional Aramaic text included, but its declaration of the nullification of vows was accurately conveyed in the paraphrased English translation. This revolutionary change in Reform liturgy and ideology can be traced back to the wave of unabashedly positive feelings toward ethnic identity, traditional observance, and meaningful ritual that washed across America in the 1960s and was crystallized in the 1976 Reform Judaism Centenary Perspective.

13

Conclusion

The quest to shed light upon the origin, development, and history of *kol nidrei* has compelled research into many unexpected and surprising fields—from vows to legal fictions, from prayer to incantations, from demons to magic bowls.

Like a detective mystery, the study of *kol nidrei* has been a process of patiently putting together the pieces of a puzzle. *Kol nidrei* cannot be adequately understood without first comprehending how the constituent pieces of this puzzle fit together: (1) the mundane, religious, and magical role of vows in the biblical and rabbinic periods; (2) the attraction of demons to carry out vows, curses, blessings, and oaths; (3) the use of magical incantations to bind the will of demons, angels, and other spirits to perform human bidding by forcing them to swear vows and oaths; (4) the talmudic procedures for the nullification of vows *ab initio* and the anticipatory invalidation of future vows; and (5) the linguistic and conceptual parallels between *kol nidrei* and the Babylonian magic bowl inscriptions.

Our sages recognized the inevitability that not all vows would be completed. They understood that human beings are far from perfect. There are people who purposefully renege on their vows. Others inadvertently forget, or extenuating circumstances arise. Still others will make rash and careless vows that they can't possibly fulfill.

Our sages understood that something had to be done to save people from themselves and from divine punishment. Without the authority to revoke vows, the rabbis instead created a legal fiction whereby vows could be annulled after the fact. They instituted a system of strict rules. No one can absolve oneself of one's own vow. Only a rabbi or a *beit din* can do it. The vow must be specified to the rabbi or *beit din*. The sages ruled that the simple regret at having made a vow is not a sufficiently compelling reason to absolve the person of it. What is critical, they believed, is one's intent. And so the rabbis insisted that there must be some unconsidered fact, circumstance, or consequence such that the vower could truthfully say, "Had I known this, I would not have made this vow."

Our sages also developed a legal formula by which some vows could retroactively be made null and void, as if they had never been. *Kol nidrei* is one such formula. *Kol nidrei* is a retroactive nullification of vows whose purpose was to spare people the dire consequences that would otherwise ensue from having failed to follow through on their vows.

There are many legends about *kol nidrei* that ought to be dispelled. *Kol nidrei* was not invented in the Middle Ages by the Marranos during the Spanish Inquisition. That is a complete myth. *Kol nidrei* had already been around for hundreds of years. It dates back to the eighth century at the very least, and possibly even before that. It probably originated in Babylonia. The Ashkenazic text refers to future vows. The *kol nidrei* of Jews from Spain and Portugal refers to past vows. The *kol nidrei* of oriental Jews incorporates the language of both.

There were other versions of *kol nidrei* in antiquity as well. *Kol nidrei* is not a prayer. It does not ask God for forgiveness or absolution. The text simply asserts it. One of the most fascinating discoveries is that there exists another *kol nidrei* from the tenth century that clearly is a penitential prayer. It directly asks God to forgive and to grant absolution.

Kol nidrei was an extremely popular ritual with the Jewish populace of ninth-century Babylonia and Palestine. It may come, then, as a surprise to learn that *kol nidrei* has been a source of controversy throughout its history, with many rabbis throughout the ages seeking to end its practice and to eliminate it from the *Machzor*. In fact, the principal reason we still have *kol nidrei* at all is because the laity refused to let it go.

Why did the rabbis of late antiquity, known as the *Geonim*, disapprove of *kol nidrei*? Publicly, they objected to it on the grounds that *kol nidrei* did not comply with all the talmudic requirements for a valid nullification of vows. And that's true. But it was really something else about *kol nidrei* that bothered them most.

In the popular Jewish imagination, *kol nidrei* did far more than annul human vows. *Kol nidrei* was a magical incantation. Its words possessed magical power to nullify the curses and hostile spells people angrily conjured against each other on a regular basis. *Kol nidrei* is a concatenation of words that neutralized the power of demons and other evil spirits, who were the enforcers of curses, to prevent them from carrying out their harmful mission.

It was precisely this effort to control and to order divine spirits to do human bidding to which the *Geonim* objected. They saw the use of magic as an affront to God's sovereignty. God's favor shouldn't be coerced. It should be earned through the power of prayer and good deeds. But the fine points of divine–human protocol were not that important to the average person. What he or she cared about was a way to guarantee, to even compel, God's help in time of crisis. And that is probably the reason why the Jewish public chose an incantational version of *kol nidrei* over a penitential one.

Yet the language of *kol nidrei* seems so heavily anchored in the mundane rather than the magical. From where did *kol nidrei*'s arcane meaning come? The solution to the mystery of *kol nidrei*'s secret meaning came in the mid-nineteenth century, when archaeologists found in Babylonia more than 100 small earthenware bowls. Written in black ink on the exterior and interior surface of these clay dishes the size of a cereal bowl were incantations that nullified curses, spells, and charms.

The remarkable discovery was that these incantation texts closely paralleled the structure and language of *kol nidrei*. They were also written in the same style as a legal nullification of vows. Many of the Aramaic words that appear in *kol nidrei* are also found in the incantation texts—including the very words *kol nidrei!*

These magic bowl incantation texts showed that the language of *kol nidrei* operated on two levels. The terminology for the various types of human vows, when transposed into a magical key, had a radically different meaning. For example, the word *neder* means "vow." But in the magical texts it means "curse." *Isar* means "prohibitive vow," but in the incantation formula it means "spell."

The implication of all this is that *kol nidrei*'s original meaning may have been completely misunderstood for centuries. While to us its language appears to refer solely to the nullification of human vows, a person from the eighth century would likely have grasped its dual meaning—that *kol nidrei* refers instead, or perhaps simultaneously, to the nullification of curses and spells. To use a musical analogy, *kol nidrei* is a sonata and we've been playing it all along in the wrong key.

There are two possible ways to understand *kol nidrei*'s original purpose. One possibility is that *kol nidrei* operated simultaneously in two keys, both the mundane and the magical. *Kol nidrei* annulled human vows and the whole range of curses we bring on ourselves and others. A second possibility is that *kol nidrei* operated only in a magical key. It nullified all these curses and had nothing to do with human vows at all. Perhaps further research will prove which theory is correct. What is most significant is that in either case, *kol nidrei* protected human beings from the harm we do to ourselves and to each other.

By the Middle Ages, *kol nidrei*'s magical dimension was lost. As the center of Jewry shifted from Babylonia to Europe, its original meaning was no longer understood. Instead, a new controversy came to the fore. Did *kol nidrei* have authority to nullify interpersonal vows? Or was it limited to vows one makes with God and imposes upon oneself?

The second *kol nidrei* debate was provoked by the great twelfth-century French Jewish sage, Jacob ben Meir, affectionately known as Rabbenu Tam. He argued that *kol nidrei* could not possibly be a retroactive nullification of vows because it failed to fulfill any of the three talmudic requirements cited earlier.

Having no desire to do away with *kol nidrei*, Rabbenu Tam proposed that the problem could be easily resolved by understanding *kol nidrei* to refer to future vows, whose annulment had no talmudic restrictions. So Rabbenu Tam emended the *kol nidrei* text to the future tense.

Rabbenu Tam's emendation did not go unchallenged. Many distinguished rabbis rose to defend *kol nidrei*'s status as a retroactive nullification of vows. It took about 500 years for Rabbenu Tam's emendation to be widely accepted by Ashkenazic Jews. But to this day it has never been accepted by the Jews of Spain and Portugal. The *kol nidrei* of oriental Jews incorporates language for both past and future vows.

Rabbenu Tam may have sought to do far more than clarify *kol nidrei*'s proper legal status. His emendation came in the context of a Jewish public that generally ascribed to *kol nidrei* sweeping powers to annul all vows—including vows made before a court, to the government, and in commercial transactions. Many of Rabbenu Tam's contemporaries and successors repeatedly tried to persuade the Jewish public that *kol nidrei* did not have the power to annul vows beyond those made with God or imposed upon oneself.

By identifying *kol nidrei* as an anticipatory invalidation of future vows, Rabbenu Tam clearly limited its legal authority. In one deft stroke, Rabbenu Tam probably sought to prove once and for all to the laity, and even to some in the rabbinic community, that *kol nidrei* does not and cannot annul interpersonal obligations.

By the early nineteenth century, many Jews had begun to view *kol nidrei* as an embarrassment, a custom that led Gentiles to believe that Jews were untrustworthy. Hadn't *kol nidrei* been responsible, they argued, for the creation in the Middle Ages of the detested and degrading *More Judaico*? The *More Judaico* was a special oath that compelled Jews to swear that they would not use *kol nidrei* or a *beit din* to recant the testimony they had offered under oath in Christian courts of law.

Declaring *kol nidrei* to be a practice that fostered prejudice against Jews and threatened their newly won acceptance into Gentile society, both lay leaders and rabbis called for *kol nidrei*'s elimination from the prayer book. In 1844, the Reform movement officially abrogated the recitation of *kol nidrei*. But this third controversy about *kol nidrei* was not limited to Reform. Even Samson Raphael Hirsch, the founder of modern Orthodoxy, temporarily eliminated *kol nidrei* from his High Holy Day services.

In place of *kol nidrei* rabbis substituted psalms or hymns, most of which continued to be sung to the *kol nidrei* melody. Some rabbis wrote new prayers that called not for the abolition of vows, but for their fulfillment. And despite the official ban, many congregations in both Europe and America continued to chant *kol nidrei* itself, albeit without offering a text or translation of its meaning. A movement to restore *kol nidrei* within Reform Judaism began in 1934. But the *kol nidrei* text and its accurate translation were not officially reinstated in the Reform movement until 1978.

Our investigation into the history of *kol nidrei* in the Geonic, Medieval, and Modern periods has revealed three intriguing patterns:

1. *Each Jewish generation gave kol nidrei a different meaning and significance.* While *kol nidrei* itself remained constant, each Jewish generation perceived it through the lenses of its own principal cultural rubric. First viewed in the Geonic period as a magical formula, *kol nidrei* was seen in the Medieval period as a legal document. In the modern period, *kol nidrei* is seen as a moving ritual, expressive of both personal spirituality and ethnic identity. This suggests that a ritual stays alive to the extent that each successive generation is able to meaningfully reinterpret the ritual in terms of its own value system. Each generation "reinvents" the ritual's meaning.

2. *Kol nidrei has been a source of controversy throughout its history.* Many rabbis throughout the ages sought to end its practice and eliminate it from the *Machzor*. The principal reason we have *kol nidrei* at all is because the laity refused to let it go. Evaluated in each generation by different standards of truth, *kol nidrei* engendered a rift between the laity and the rabbinate in all three of the historical periods we researched.

In the Geonic period, the *kol nidrei* debate revolved around the proper limits of magic in monotheistic religion. The debate shifted in the Middle Ages to the issue of *kol nidrei*'s legal authority: what is permitted and what is forbidden. In the early modern period, the *kol nidrei* debate centered on the distinction between its substantive content and the *kol nidrei* melody. The debate over *kol nidrei* in the late modern period has centered on meaningful versus nonmeaningful ritual.[1]

3. *In every era, Jews were drawn to kol nidrei because of something other that its intellectual content.* Paradoxically, the folk have never been drawn to *kol nidrei*'s substantive content but to the power with which they invested it. While the *kol nidrei* formula in the Geonic period ostensibly refers to human vows, folk religion construed it to refer to demons. Although their *poskim* told them otherwise, the folk in the Middle Ages invested *kol nidrei* with the power to annul solemn promises made to others. In the modern period, while the rabbis for the most part sought ideological purity, the folk endowed the *kol nidrei* melody and its exotic Aramaic language with haunting emotional power.

---

1. *Kol nidrei*'s history basically reflects the three types of truth that Hoffman refers to as the limits game, the truth game, and the meaning game. See Lawrence Hoffman, "Jewish Knowledge: Redrawing the Map," *Conservative Judaism* 38 (Winter 1985–1986): 36–43.

Epilogue

We have now completed our journey into the true story of *kol nidrei*. We understand so much more about its origin, development, and history. We better understand its meaning and can appreciate its profound significance to prior Jewish generations. But what, then, can *kol nidrei* mean for us today?

Let us not be put off by our ancestors' literal belief in demons and evil spirits, curses and magic spells. These concepts have lost none of their metaphoric truth. Are we not also haunted at midnight by the demons of regret and guilt? Have we not brought a curse upon ourselves by the consequences of our misdeeds and foolish choices? Does not *kol nidrei* magically bestow upon us a few moments of protected time to stop and reflect upon the meaning and direction of our lives? Our ancestors were not so primitive. We are not so advanced. Despite the centuries, their fears and ours, our hopes and theirs, remain the same.

Kol nidrei teaches us something about the great power of religious ritual. Intellect alone cannot inspire us to do what we ought. Nor can it help us to fully mourn our losses and get on with life. It is ritual that gives us the emotional closure we yearn for. It is through ritual that we come into contact with our deepest selves. The profoundly meaningful role that Jewish ritual can play in our lives should never be underestimated.

Judaism accords great respect to the power of words, for God created the world through words. "And God *said*, 'Let there be light.' And there was light." As the most highly valued and powerful words one can speak, the making of vows and oaths is taken very seriously in Judaism. Both biblical and rabbinic texts exhort people to fulfill their vows, and for good reason. The foundation stone upon which all civilized society depends is that a person's word must be his or her bond. We live in a society where words are cheap and the volume of litigation is unprecedented. Our Judaism reminds us that our word can and must be our bond. What we vow, we must fulfill. This is what God requires of us. This is the way of holiness.

The Torah takes vows so seriously that it has no provision, with one exception, for the revocation of vows. It was universally accepted in antiquity that a vow, once uttered, could not be taken back. It was operative and in force, independent of human control. By analogy, it is like the aftermath of having put one's foot in one's mouth. Desperately we want to take those words back. But it's too late. The damage has been done.

The making of vows was an extremely dangerous business, not to be taken lightly, and never to be toyed with. The sincere individual who had failed to fulfill a vow because of unintentional neglect or because of some compelling circumstance, or the person who made a careless or rash vow that could not or should not be carried through found themselves in a grave situation, facing not only divine displeasure but also certain punishment from a self-inflicted curse. And that is why, to this very day, it is a Jewish custom when making a promise to add *beli neder*—"this is not a vow!"

A rabbinic story tells how Rabbi Shimon ben Gamliel once told his servant, Tevi, to buy the best food in the market. The servant bought tongue. He then instructed his servant to buy the worst food in the market. Tevi again bought tongue. Rabbi Gamliel said to him, "What is this? When I asked you to get the best food, you bought me tongue. When I asked you to buy me the worst food, you also bought me tongue!" Tevi replied, "Both good and bad come through the tongue. When the tongue is good, there is nothing better. When it's bad, there is nothing worse" (*Vayikra Rabbah* 33:1).

The words we choose to say or not say can open doors or shut them, build bridges or burn them. More than 30 percent of the *al cheit* prayer, that great communal confession of sin recited on Yom Kippur, refers to the sins of human speech. *Kol nidrei* speaks to the power of words to heal or hurt. We must become more careful with our words.

Kol nidrei speaks to the sad truth of how we treat each other and ourselves at our worst. It gives us the courage to admit that we have sinned against each other both intentionally and unwittingly.

> *Al chet shechantanu lefanekha.*
> For the sin of treating others with arrogance and contempt
> For the sin of being overly critical and judgmental with others
>   and ourselves
> For the sin of acting in bad faith and bearing ill will
> For the sin of being insensitive to the needs of others
> For the sin of bearing grudges
> For the sin of not having adequate compassion for the weak-
>   nesses of others and ourselves
> For the sin of wanting always to be right rather than stay close

Are these not the ways in which we curse each other? Are these not the ways that we send demons to hurt each other for having been hurt? *Kol nidrei* spares us from having to pay the full price for these failures and misdeeds. It spares us, not by letting us off the hook, but by giving us another chance to do better. *Kol nidrei* leaves us feeling dissatisfied with who we are. Could we not be more kind? Yes! Gentle? Yes! More involved? Yes! More charitable? Yes!

Kol nidrei teaches us that when the High Holy Days are over, our work really begins. Now is the time for truth. Now is the time to ask ourselves hard questions. *Kol nidrei* grants us a new beginning, a fresh opportunity to bring blessing into the lives of our families and our synagogue community.

Appendix I
Versions of *Kol Nidrei*

1. THE ASHKENAZI *KOL NIDREI* FORMULA[1]

כָּל נִדְרֵי וֶאֱסָרֵי וַחֲרָמֵי וְקוֹנָמֵי וְכִנּוּיֵי וְקִנּוּסֵי וּשְׁבוּעֵי ‹נ"א וּשְׁבוּעוֹת›

דְּנָדַרְנָא וּדְאִשְׁתְּבַּעְנָא וּדְאַחֲרִימְנָא וְדַאֲסַרְנָא עַל נַפְשָׁתָנָא

נוסח ישן, וברוב הקהלות משמיטין אותו

[מִיּוֹם כִּפּוּרִים שֶׁעָבַר עַד יוֹם כִּפּוּרִים זֶה]

מִיּוֹם כִּפּוּרִים זֶה עַד יוֹם כִּפּוּרִים הַבָּא עָלֵינוּ לְטוֹבָה.

5   כֻּלְּהוֹן אִחֲרַטְנָא בְהוֹן. כֻּלְּהוֹן יְהוֹן שָׁרַן.

שְׁבִיקִין שְׁבִיתִין. בְּטֵלִין וּמְבֻטָּלִין.

לָא שְׁרִירִין וְלָא קַיָּמִין:

נִדְרָנָא לָא נִדְרֵי. בד"ס מוסיפין וֶאֱסָרָנָא לָא אֱסָרֵי

וּשְׁבוּעֲתָנָא לָא שְׁבוּעוֹת:

[ככתוב בתורת משה עבדך מפי כבודך]

10 וְנִסְלַח לְכָל עֲדַת בְּנֵי יִשְׂרָאֵל וְלַגֵּר הַגָּר בְּתוֹכָם כִּי לְכָל הָעָם בִּשְׁגָגָה: ‹נ"ס›

---

1. From Daniel Goldschmidt, ed., *Machzor laYamim haNoraim* (New York: Leo Baeck Institute, 1970), p. 1.

בסנג אלין נהגין להוסיף

(ח) סְלַח־נָא לַעֲוֹן הָעָם הַזֶּה כְּגֹדֶל חַסְדֶּךָ וְכַאֲשֶׁר נָשָׂאתָ לָעָם הַזֶּה מִמִּצְרַיִם וְעַד־הֵנָּה: וְשָׁם נֶאֱמַר.

(ק) וַיֹּאמֶר יְיָ סָלַחְתִּי כִּדְבָרֶךָ: (ג־ס)

בָּרוּךְ אַתָּה יְיָ אֱלֹהֵינוּ מֶלֶךְ הָעוֹלָם שֶׁהֶחֱיָנוּ וְקִיְּמָנוּ וְהִגִּיעָנוּ לַזְּמַן הַזֶּה:

2. THE WESTERN SEPHARDI
KOL NIDREI FORMULA[2]

ושלש פעמים החכם אומר כל נדרי להתיר לאדם מהמשה שעברה את הנדרים הנוגעים לו לבדו. איגו מתיר בשם אוסן את הנדרים הנוגעים לחברו או למי שהוא מלבדו

כָּל־נִדְרֵי. וֶאֱסָרֵי. וּשְׁבוּעֵי. וַחֲרָמֵי. וְנִדּוּיֵי. וְקוּנָּמֵי. וְקִנּוּחֵי. וְקִנּוּסֵי. דִּי נְדַרְנָא. וְדִי אִשְׁתַּבַּעְנָא. וְדִי חֲרַמְנָא. וְדִי נָדֵינָא. וְדִי אָסַרְנָא עַל נַפְשָׁתָנָא. מִיּוֹם הַכִּפֻּרִים שֶׁעָבַר. עַד יוֹם הַכִּפֻּרִים הַזֶּה. **שֶׁבָּא עָלֵינוּ לְשָׁלוֹם:

והקהל עונין

נְדָרִינָא לָא נִדְרֵי. וּשְׁבוּעָנָא לָא שְׁבוּעֵי. חֲרָמָנָא לָא חֲרָמֵי. וְנִדּוּיִינָא לָא נִדּוּיֵי. וַאֲסָרְנָא לָא אֱסָרֵי: כֻּלְּהוֹן יְהוֹן שְׁבִיתִין. וּשְׁבִיקִין. לָא שְׁרִירִין. וְלָא קַיָּמִין: תִּסְלַח לְכָל־עֲדַת בְּנֵי יִשְׂרָאֵל. וְלַגֵּר הַגָּר בְּתוֹכָם. כִּי לְכָל־הָעָם בִּשְׁגָגָה:

הש"ץ מברך

בָּרוּךְ אַתָּה יְיָ. אֱלֹהֵינוּ מֶלֶךְ הָעוֹלָם. שֶׁהֶחֱיָנוּ. וְקִיְּמָנוּ. וְהִגִּיעָנוּ לַזְּמַן הַזֶּה:

---

2. From David de Sola Pool, *Prayers for the Day of Atonement: According to the Custom of the Spanish and Portuguese Jews* (New York: Union of Sephardic Congregations, 1984), p. 26.

3. THE ORIENTAL SEPHARDI
KOL NIDREI FORMULA

כָּל נִדְרֵי. וֶאֱסָרֵי. וּשְׁבוּעֵי. וְנִדּוּיֵי. וַחֲרָמֵי. וְקוּנָמֵי. וְקוּנָחֵי.

וְקוּנָסֵי. דִּי נְדַרְנָא. וְדִי נִנְדַּר. דִּי אִשְׁתְּבַעְנָא. וְדִי נִשְׁתְּבַע.

דִּי נַדֵּינָא. וְדִי נְנַדֵּי. דִּי חֲרַמְנָא. וְדִי נַחֲרִים. דִּי אֲסַרְנָא עַל

נַפְשָׁתָנָא. וְדִי נֶאֱסַר. מִיּוֹם הַכִּפּוּרִים שֶׁעָבַר. עַד יוֹם

הַכִּפּוּרִים הַזֶּה שֶׁבָּא עָלֵינוּ לְשָׁלוֹם. וּמִיּוֹם הַכִּפּוּרִים הַזֶּה

עַד יוֹם הַכִּפּוּרִים שֶׁיָּבֹא עָלֵינוּ לְשָׁלוֹם. נִדְרָנָא לָא נִדְרֵי.

וּשְׁבוּעֶנָא לָא שְׁבוּעֵי. וְנִדּוּיֵינָא לָא נִדּוּיֵי. וַחֲרָמְנָא לָא

חֲרָמֵי. וֶאֱסָרָנָא לָא אֱסָרֵי. כֻּלְּהוֹן אִתְחָרַטְנָא בְהוֹן. יְהֵא

רַעֲוָא דִּי יְהוֹן שְׁבִיתִין וּשְׁבִיקִין. לָא שְׁרִירִין וְלָא קַיָּמִין.

וְנִסְלַח לְכָל עֲדַת בְּנֵי יִשְׂרָאֵל וְלַגֵּר הַגָּר בְּתוֹכָם. כִּי

לְכָל־הָעָם בִּשְׁגָגָה:

Appendix II
The Music of *Kol Nidrei* among *Ashkenazim* and *Sephardim*

1. A YEMENITE *KOL NIDREI*[1]

---

1. From A. Z. Idelsohn, *Thesaurus of Hebrew Oriental Melodies*, vol. 1 (New York: Ktav, 1933), pp. 57–58.

149

'ȧḏ jôm häk̲.kip.pu. rim šä. jo. b̲ô̲   'o. lê. nu lĕ̲. šo. lôm

niḏ. ro. no lo niḏ̲.rêj uš.b̲u. 'o. t̲o. no lo šĕ.b̲u.'êj wå.h̲ä̲.ro.

mä.no lo h̲ä̲.ro.mêj wĕ.nid.du.jä̲.no lo nid.du jêj   wä. ä̲.so.rå.no

lo ä̲.so.rêj kul. hôn it̲. h̲ä̲.råt̲.no bŏ̲.hôn jĕ̲.hêj rå̲.wo di.hôn

šĕ̲. b̲i. t̲in uš. b̲i. gin   lo šä̲.ri. rin wĕ. lo gåj. jo. min

wĕ̲.nis. låh̲ lĕ̲. h̲ol å̲. dät̲ bĕ̲. nêj jis. ro. êl wĕ̲.läǧ.ǧêr häǧ.ǧor

bĕ̲. t̲ô. h̲om   kij lĕ̲.h̲ol ho. 'om   biš.ǧo. ǧoh.

2. A PERSIAN KOL NIDREI[2]

Ko.lĕ ni.dĕ̲.rêj wä.ä̲.so. rêj   u.šĕ̲.wu.êj   wĕ̲.ni. du. jêj

wa.h̲ä̲. ro. mêj   wĕ̲.kû. no. mêj   wĕ̲.kû no. h̲êj   wĕ̲.kû. no. sêj.

di nĕ̲dar.no wĕ̲di nin. dar,   di iš.ta.ba.no wĕ̲di. niš. ta   . ba.

di nĕ̲.dêj. no wĕ̲di   nin. dêj, di h̲ä̲.ram.no wĕ̲di   nä.h̲ä̲.ram,

di ä̲.sar. no wĕ̲di   nä.ä̲. sar al naf.šo.t̲o. no mi.jûm ki.pu.rim

2. From A. Z. Idelsohn, *Thesaurus of Hebrew Oriental Melodies*, vol. 3 (New York: Ktav, 1933), p. 35.

3. AN ORIENTAL SEPHARDI *KOL NIDREI*[3]

3. From A. Z. Idelsohn, *Thesaurus of Hebrew Oriental Melodies*, vol. 4 (New York: Ktav, 1933), p. 217.

4. A MOROCCAN *KAL NIDREI*[4]

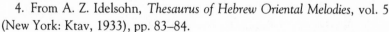

---

4. From A. Z. Idelsohn, *Thesaurus of Hebrew Oriental Melodies*, vol. 5 (New York: Ktav, 1933), pp. 83–84.

sĕ‿bi‿ṭin   us‿bi‿'in   la sĕ‿ri‿rin wĕ‿lô àj‿ja‿min.   wĕ‿nis‿laḥ lĕ‿ḥol 'ă‿daṭ

bĕ‿nê jis‿ra‿êl wĕ‿lag‿gêr hag‿gar bĕ‿ṭô‿ham, ki lĕ‿ḥol ha‿'am   bis‿ga‿ga.

5. THE AARON BEER *KOL NIDREI* (1765)[5]

---

5. From A. Z. Idelsohn, "The Kol Nidre Tune," *HUCA* 8–9 (1931–1932): 493–509.

6. THE S. NAUMBOURG *KOL NIDREI*
(1840–1874)[6]

6. From A. Z. Idelsohn, "The Kol Nidre Tune," *HUCA* 8–9 (1931–1932): 493–509.

7. THE L. LEWANDOWSKI *KOL NIDREI* (1871)[7]

---

7. From A. Z. Idelsohn, "The Kol Nidre Tune," *HUCA* 8–9 (1931–1932): 493–509.

8. THE ABRAHAMS BAER *KOL NIDREI* (1877)[8]

---

8. From A. Z. Idelsohn, "The Kol Nidre Tune," *HUCA* 8–9 (1931–1932): 493–509.

Selected Bibliography

RABBINIC SOURCES

Abudarham haShalem. Ed. S. A. Wertheimer. Jerusalem, 1963.

Arba'ah Turim, Orach Chayyim, Hilkhot Yom haKippurim 619.

Arugat haBosem. Ed. Ephraim Urbach. Jerusalem, 1967.

Machzor Vitry. Ed. Simon haLevi Hurwitz. Nuremberg: Mekitsei Nirdamim, 1923.

Mishneh Torah, Sefer Hafla'ah, Hilkhot Shevuot and Nedarim.

Orchot Chayyim. 1750. Reprint. Jerusalem, 1956.

Otsar haGeonim. Ed. Benjamin Lewin. Vol. 11. Palestine, 1942.

Rosh to *Yoma* 88 end, #28.

Seder Rav Amram Gaon. Ed. Daniel Goldschmidt. Jerusalem: Mossad haRav Kook, 1971.

Sefer haManhig. 1856. Reprint. Jerusalem, 1967.

Sefer haYashar. 1811. Reprint. Brooklyn: Shai Publications, 1959.

Sefer Levush, Orach Chayyim, Hilkhot Yom Kippur #619.

Sefer Maharil. Warsaw, 1802.

Sefer Ravyah. Ed. Avigdor Aptowitzer. Part 2. Jerusalem: Harry Fischel Institute, 1964.

Sha'arei Simchah. Ed. Simchah Bamberger. Vol 1. Furth, 1861.

Sha'arei Teshuvah. Ed. Wolf Leiter. 1802. Reprint. New York: Philipp Feldheim, 1946.

She'elot uTeshuvot haRibash #394.

Shibbolei haLeket. Ed. Solomon Buber. 1886. Reprint. Jerusalem: Alef Publishing Company, 1962.

Shulchan Arukh, Orach Chayyim, Hilkhot Yom haKippurim #619.

Siddur Rabbenu Shlomo. Ed. Moshe Hershler. Jerusalem, 1971.

Teshuvot, Pesakim uMinhagim shel Maharam. Ed. I. Z. Cahana. Vol 1. Jerusalem: Mossad haRav Kook, 1957.

OTHER SOURCES

Abramson, Shraga. "Early Rulings" [Hebrew]. *Sinai* 49 (1961): 210–215.

———. "On the Blessing for the Nullification of Vows and Oaths" [Hebrew]. *Sinai* 50 (1962): 185–186.

Ahituv, Shmuel. "Azazel." *Encyclopaedia Judaica.* Ed. Cecil Roth and Geoffrey Wigoder. Jerusalem: Keter Publishing House, 1972.

Albeck, Chanoch, ed. *Shishah Sidrei Mishnah. Seder Nashim. Masekhet Nedarim.* Jerusalem: Mossad Bialik, 1959.

Avineri, Hanoch. "Mi-Sinai Niggunim." *Encyclopaedia Judaica.* Ed. Cecil Roth and Geoffrey Wigoder. Jerusalem: Keter Publishing House, 1972.

Azar, Moshe. *Leshonot Hitchayavut beMikra uveMishnah.* [Expressions of Commitments in the Old Testament and in the Mishnah]. Haifa: Pinat haSefer, 1981.

Baron, Salo. *A Social and Religious History of the Jews.* Vols. 5–8. New York: Columbia University Press, 1957–1958.

Bayer, Bathja. "Kol Nidre." *Encyclopaedia Judaica.* Ed. Cecil Roth and Geoffrey Wigoder. Jerusalem: Keter Publishing House, 1972.

Beyerlin, Walter. *Near Eastern Religious Texts Relating to the Old Testament.* Philadelphia: Westminster Press, 1978.

Buchanan, George Wesley. "Some Vow and Oath Formulas in the New Testament." *Harvard Theological Review* 58 (July 1965): 319–326.

Budd, Philip J. *Numbers.* Word Biblical Commentary. Vol. 5. Waco: Word Book, 1984.

CCAR Yearbook 40 (1930): 100–108.

CCAR Yearbook 41 (1931): 102–115.

CCAR Yearbook 55 (1945): 33–34.

Cohen, Francis. "Kol Nidre." The Jewish Encyclopedia. Ed. Isadore Singer. New York: Funk and Wagnalls Co., 1916.

Concise Encyclopedia of Jewish Music, 1975 ed. S.v. "Kol Nidre."

Danby, Herbert. The Mishnah. London: Oxford University Press, 1933.

Davidson, Israel. "Kol Nidre." American Jewish Yearbook 25 (1923): 180–194.

de Vaux, Roland. Ancient Israel: Its Life and Institutions. London: Darton, Longman & Todd, 1961.

Deshen, Shlomo. "The Enigma of Kol Nidre: An Anthropological and Historical Approach." In Studies in the History of Jewish Society in the Middle Ages and in the Modern Period: Presented to Professor Jacob Katz, ed. E. Etkes and Y. Salmon, 136–153. Jerusalem: Magnes Press, 1980.

Encyclopedia of the Jewish Religion, 1966 ed. S.v. "Vows and Oaths."

Encyclopedia of the Jewish Religion, 1966 ed., S.v. "Demonology."

Encyclopedia Talmudit, 2nd rev. ed., 1973. S. v. "Hatarat Nedarim."

Falk, Ze'ev. "On Talmudic Vows." Harvard Theological Review 59 (July 1966): 309–312.

———. Introduction to Jewish Law of the Second Commonwealth. Leiden: E. J. Brill, 1972.

———. "Binding and Loosing." In Studies in Jewish Legal History: Essays in Honour of David Daube, ed. Bernard Jackson, 92–100. London: Jewish Chronicle Publications, 1974.

Friedland, Eric. "The Historical and Theological Development of the Non-Orthodox Prayerbooks in the United States," Ph.D. diss., Brandeis University, 1967.

Ginzberg, Louis. Ginzei Schecter. Vol 2. Reprint. New York: Jewish Theological Seminary, 1929.

Gordon, Cyrus H. "Aramaic Incantation Bowls." Orientalia 10 (1941): 116.

———. "Leviathan: Symbol of Evil." In Biblical Motifs Origins and

Transformations, ed. Alexander Altmann, 1–9. Cambridge, MA: Harvard University Press, 1966.

Gray, George Buchanan. *Sacrifice in the Old Testament: Its Theory and Practice*. New York: Ktav, 1971.

Greenberg, Moshe. "Oaths." *Encyclopaedia Judaica*. Eds. Cecil Roth and Geoffrey Wigoder. Jerusalem: Keter Publishing House, 1972.

Harper's Bible Dictionary, 8th ed. S.v. "Vow."

Heller, Joseph. *Isaac M. Wise: His Life, Work and Thought*. New York, 1965.

Herr, Moshe David. "Matters of Palestinian *Halakhah* During the Sixth and Seventh Centuries CE" [Hebrew]. *Tarbiz* 48 (October 1979–March 1980): 62–80.

Hoffman, Lawrence A. *The Canonization of the Synagogue Service*. Notre Dame, IN: University of Notre Dame Press, 1979.

———. *Gates of Understanding Two*. New York: Central Conference of American Rabbis, 1984.

———. "Jewish Knowledge: Redrawing the Map." *Conservative Judaism* 38 (Winter 1985-1986): 36–43.

Idelsohn, A. Z. "The Kol Nidre Tune." *Hebrew Union College Annual* 8–9 (1931–1932): 493–503.

———. *Thesaurus of Hebrew Oriental Melodies*. Vols. 6–7. New York: Ktav, 1933.

Kieval, Herman. "The Curious Case of *Kol Nidre*." *Commentary* 46 (October 1968): 53–58.

Kohler, Kaufman. "Demonology." *The Jewish Encyclopedia*. Ed. Isadore Singer. New York: Funk and Wagnalls Co., 1916.

Levine, Baruch A. "Appendix: The Language of the Magic Bowls." In Jacob Neusner, *A History of the Jews in Babylonia*, vol. 5, 343–387. Leiden: E. J. Brill, 1970.

———. *In the Presence of the Lord*. Leiden: E. J. Brill, 1974.

Lieberman, Saul. *Greek in Jewish Palestine*. New York: Jewish Theological Seminary of America, 1942.

———. *Texts and Studies*. New York: Ktav, 1974.

Long, Bruce J. "Demons." *The Encyclopedia of Religion*. Ed. Mircea Eliade. New York: Macmillan Publishing Co., 1987.

Ludwig, Theodore M. "Incantations." *The Encyclopedia of Religion*. Ed. Mircea Eliade. New York: Macmillan Publishing Co., 1987.

Mann, Jacob. *Texts and Studies in Jewish History and Literature*. 2 vols. Cincinnati: Hebrew Union College Press, 1931.

Margaliot, Mordechai. *Halakhot Erets Yisrael Min haGenizah*. Jerusalem: Mossad haRav Kook, 1973.

Mendes-Flohr, Paul, and Reinharz, Jehuda, eds., *The Jew in the Modern World: A Documentary History*. New York: Oxford University Press, 1980.

Meyer, Michael A. *Response to Modernity*. New York: Oxford University Press, 1988.

Milgrom, Jacob. "Day of Atonement." *Encyclopaedia Judaica*. Ed. Cecil Roth and Geoffrey Wigoder. Jerusalem: Keter Publishing House, 1972.

———. "Kipper." *Encyclopaedia Judaica*. Ed. Cecil Roth and Geofrey Wigoder. Jerusalem: Keter Publishing House, 1972.

Montgomery, James A. *Aramaic Incantation Texts from Nippur*. Philadelphia: University of Pennsylvania Press, 1913.

Neusner, Jacob. "The Phenomenon of the Rabbi in Late Antiquity." *Numen* 16 (April 1969): 1–20.

———. *A History of the Jews in Babylonia*. Vols. 5–6. Leiden: E. J. Brill, 1970.

Noth, Martin. *Leviticus: A Commentary*. The Old Testament Library. Philadelphia: Westminster Press, 1965.

———. *Numbers: A Commentary*. The Old Testament Library. Philadelphia: Westminster Press, 1968.

Petuchowski, Jakob. *Prayerbook Reform in Europe*. New York: The World Union for Progressive Judaism, 1968.

Philipson, David. *The Reform Movement in Judaism*. New York: Ktav, 1967.

Plaut, Gunther. *The Rise of Reform Judaism*. New York: World Union for Progressive Judaism, 1963.

Rabinovitch, Mordechai. *The Mishnah: Seder Nashim Vol. II(a) Tractate Nedarim*. ArtScroll Mishnah Series. Brooklyn: Mesorah Publications, 1985.

Rabinowitz, Louis Isaac. "Vows and Vowing." *Encyclopaedia Judaica*. Ed. Cecil Roth and Geoffrey Wigoder. Jerusalem: Keter Publishing House, 1972.

Raphael, Marc Lee. *Profiles in American Judaism*. New York: Harper & Row, 1984.

Rosenbloom, Noah H. *Tradition in an Age of Reform*. Philadelphia: Jewish Publication Society, 1976.

Rossell, William H. *A Handbook of Aramaic Magical Texts*. Shelton Semitic Series Number II. Ringwood Borough, NJ: Shelton College, 1953.

Seltzer, Robert M. *Jewish People. Jewish Thought: The Jewish Experience in History*. New York: Macmillan Publishing Co., 1980.

Sendrey, Alfred. *The Music of the Jews in the Diaspora*. New York: Thomas Yoseloff, 1970.

Snaith, N. H., ed. *Leviticus and Numbers*. The Century Bible. London: Thoms Nelson & Sons, 1967.

Spector, Johanna. "The Kol Nidre—At Least 1200 Years Old." *Jewish Music Notes* (October 1950): 3–4.

Sturdy, John. *Numbers*. The Cambridge Bible Commentary. London: Cambridge University Press, 1976.

Toner, P. J. "Exorcism." *The Catholic Encyclopedia*. New York: McGraw-Hill, 1909.

Trachtenberg, Joshua. *Jewish Magic and Superstition: A Study in Folk Religion*. New York: Atheneum, 1939.

Urbach, Ephraim. *Ba'alei Tosaphot*. Jerusalem: The Bialik Institute, 1955.

Werner, Eric. *A Voice Still Heard*. University Park, PA: The Pennsylvania State University Press, 1976.

PRAYER BOOKS

The Complete ArtScroll Machzor. Ed. Nosson Scherman. Brooklyn: Mesorah Publications, 1986.

Einhorn, David. *Olat Tamid: Book of Prayers for Jewish Congregations.*
    1896.
Gates of Repentance: The New Union Prayerbook for the Days of Awe.
    Ed. Chaim Stern. New York: Central Conference of American
    Rabbis, 1978.
Machzor laYamim haNoraim. Ed. Daniel Goldschmidt. 2 vols. New
    York: Leo Baeck Institute, 1970.
Machzor Tefillah leMoshe: Lefi Minhag haSefaradim ve'Edot haMizrach.
    Ed. Moshe Rabi. Jerusalem: n.p., 1982.
*Prayers for the Day of Atonement: According to the Custom of the Span-
    ish and Portuguese Jews.* Ed. David de Sola Pool. New York:
    Union of Sephardic Congregations, 1984.
The Union Prayerbook for Jewish Worship, Part II. Cincinnati: Central
    Conference of American Rabbis, 1894.
The Union Prayerbook for Jewish Worship, Part II. Newly Revised Edi-
    tion. Cincinnati: Central Conference of American Rabbis, 1945.
Wise, Isaac M. *The Divine Service of American Israelites for the Day of
    Atonement.* Cincinnati: Bloch & Company, 1866.

Index

ABOUT THE AUTHOR

Rabbi Stuart Weinberg Gershon received rabbinic ordination and a master's degree in Hebrew literature from Hebrew Union College-Jewish Institute of Religion as well as a master's degree in Jewish education from the Jewish Theological Seminary of America. He was the chairperson of the Jewish Education Committee of the Worcester Jewish Federation and served as associate rabbi of Temple Emanuel in Worcester, Massachusetts. He is currently the spiritual leader of Temple Sinai in Summit, New Jersey. He and his wife Diana reside in the Summit, New Jersey, area with their son, Aaron Lev.